DON'T BE AFRAID . . .

Don't Be Afraid...
About Recovery from Alcoholism

by
S.A.S.

Exposition Press
Hicksville, New York

First Edition

ISBN 0-682-49061-X

Printed in the United States of America

Special Thanks

I want to say "many thanks" to a very sweet young lady who did all the typing and correcting for me, in order for this book to become reality. The lady is Miss Margaret Wangen, of Albert Lea, Minnesota.

Thanks a million, Maggie!

—The Author

TRADITION ELEVEN
of Alcoholics Anonymous

Our public relations policy is based on attraction rather than promotion; we need always maintain personal anonymity at the level of press, radio, and films.

CONTENTS

Foreword 9

Acknowledgments 11

My Story 17
My First AA Talk 23
My Second AA Talk 29
Sobriety Comes First 33
Step One 39
Step Two 51
Step Three 57
Step Four 63
Step Five 69
Step Six 75
Step Seven 79
Step Eight 83
Step Nine 87
Step Ten 91
Step Eleven 95
Step Twelve 101
The "Serenity Prayer" 107
The "Mastery" of Sobriety 113
Spirituality 121
A New Way of Living 127
Random Thoughts 133

FOREWORD

This book is not intended as a textbook or guide. My only hope is that someone who reads it will either find comfort or seek help for himself or a loved one.

I cannot represent AA, so please, as you go on reading, keep in mind that whatever is written here is only as I understand it, or as I see it, or as I think or feel. I am not an authority on alcoholism or drug dependency, but I am an alcoholic who has risen from a "skid-row existence" to find a fairly decent life on earth.

My experiences might not be unique to some, but to me they are; and my way of thinking or living might not be approved by some, but, as long as I can face myself when I look in the mirror, I am satisfied.

Keep this in mind as you read the pages, that it is only my opinions, my thoughts and ideas. I have been without a drink for many years, and it is only through the AA philosophy that I have been able to stay sober.

ACKNOWLEDGMENTS

Thanks to a lot of people, I have been able to put this book together. There are many, many people that I need to say thank you to. I name some, and to the rest of you I dedicate these pages.

Special thanks to my wife, Anna-Marie, for sticking by me even when others told her to leave me, and to our children, Ruth and Jon-Erik, who have never, thank God, seen me drunk, but have helped me with my spiritual growth.

Thank you, Tom Y. and Dick G. for endless hours that you have spent with me, as my sponsors. I am deeply grateful for your assistance, your guidance, and your support.

Thank you, God, for letting Your help come to me through people. Without my faith in You, I would not have made it. God, thank you for the days that have gone by and the days I might still have. But, most of all, thank You for *today*.

THE TWELVE STEPS
OF ALCOHOLICS ANONYMOUS

1—We admitted we were powerless over alcohol—that our lives had become unmanageable.

2—Came to believe that a Power greater than ourselves could restore us to sanity.

3—Made a decision to turn our will and our lives over to the care of God *as we understood Him.*

4—Made a searching and fearless moral inventory of ourselves.

5—Admitted to God, to ourselves and to another human being the exact nature of our wrongs.

6—Were entirely ready to have God remove all these defects of character.

7—Humbly asked Him to remove our shortcomings.

8—Made a list of all persons we had harmed, and became willing to make amends to them all.

9—Made direct amends to such people wherever possible, except when to do so would injure them or others.

10—Continued to take personal inventory and when we were wrong promptly admitted it.

11—Sought through prayer and meditation to improve our conscious contact with God, *as we understood Him,* praying only for knowledge of His will for us and the power to carry that out.

12—Having had a spiritual awakening as the result of these steps, we tried to carry this message to alcoholics, and to practice these principles in all our affairs.

DON'T BE AFRAID . . .

MY STORY

I was born in a little mining town in northern Norway, a small town, where everyone knew one another and one another's business.

My parents were working-class people, and I was the youngest of three. My parents did not use alcohol, and I have never seen my brother or sister drunk, yet both will take a social drink.

When World War II broke out and Norway was occupied by the Germans, I was just starting school. There were barbed-wire fences put up everywhere, and we had to go through six gates to get to school. German soldiers were everywhere, and at times we would ask them for candy, and, if we were not too many kids together, they would give us candy.

The Germans had placed land mines all around the mining company's offices and buildings, and guards were patrolling regularly. Every so often, mines would explode because a hare or fox had gotten into the mine field. One soldier was killed in such a mishap.

People were often stopped and searched on the way to and from work, and it was not unusual that German soldiers suddenly came to homes to search for something or someone.

Because I was still just a kid, I had not learned the seriousness of war, and, when we kids were skiing in the hills, often German soldiers were there, too, in training for their skiing skills. They were poor skiers, which we kids soon discovered, and we made fun of them by racing them on skis. We say kiddingly that up there where I came from, we are "born with skis on," because in the winter that is the only means of transportation. We also say that we have "nine months of winter and three months of poor skiing."

My father was involved in the Norwegian Underground, and

one day he somehow got the message that he had better disappear, because he was next on the Nazi's list to be executed. So, he came home from work that day and told my mother that we all would be taking off for Sweden that evening. Sweden was neutral during the war, and my father had been guiding people over the mountains into Sweden as part of his job for the Underground. He knew every rock and bush up there, and, even though there were Germans patrolling all the time, he was never caught. So, we took off for Sweden on skis. It was eight days before Christmas 1943.

In Sweden, I got to taste alcohol for the first time. It did something to me. It tickled my throat. It warmed me inside, but the amount was just tiny.

After we came back home again, in the fall of 1945, it took some time before things had settled down to "normal." I went back to school, my parents back to work. Also, my brother and sister had jobs. There were a few times when I got to taste alcohol, usually at friends' houses, but again it was just a few teaspoonfuls. The tingling feeling in my throat, the warmth and burning as I swallowed it—I got something from the taste. It did something for me.

At the age of sixteen, I had saved enough money to buy my first bottle. A guy who was over twenty-one bought the bottle for me, and I experienced my first intoxication, first blackout, and my first insane behavior outbreak. Already, from my first intoxication, I was hooked. The "bad" things that happened to me during this intoxication I did not like, but it did not stop me from wanting more alcohol.

I attended Saturday-night dances and got a few drinks here and there from guys that brought their own flasks with them. It did not take long before people began talking about me and my drinking habit.

At nineteen, I broke into our neighbor's basement and stole some homemade wine; when I tried a second trip for more wine, I was caught. Our neighbor brought me home into our kitchen, and my father slapped my face back and forth a few times, and I noticed he was crying while punishing me. His face showed hurt, anger, and shame, and there was much more hurt to come as my drinking progressed.

Luckily for me, I was drafted into the service shortly thereafter and served eighteen months in the Norwegian air force. Several times, during my service time, I spent time in the jail on our base for drunkenness.

My first drinking "bender" came about when the girl I was engaged to broke the engagement. She had tried so many times to get me to stop drinking, but all her attempts were fruitless. When she finally called it "quits," I went on a three-week drunk in a hotel in another town. The hotel owner finally called my brother, and he and my brother-in-law came and got me.

It was after this experience that my insanity really came out. I swore to "hurt" and shame as many women as I could. "Lay them and leave them" was the motto I worked by. Of course, this insanity could not go on forever either, and quite often I was too drunk. I passed out before any "hurt" could be done.

I made good money as a painter-decorator and was looked upon with respect in my trade. In sports, I was well qualified as a soccer player and was the captain of our team for six years in a row. I was chosen to play on the North Norway team to play against North Sweden, Finland, and Russia. Strange things took place at times on our trips to play the games that were scheduled. I could be dead drunk on Saturday night, but on Sunday morning I was full of "get up and go."

I met my wife at a school outside Oslo. She was one of a hundred or so American students in Scandinavia. Even before the school year was over, she was aware of my drinking problem, yet, she agreed to marry me anyway. She said later that she thought that I would "straighten out" when we got married and I got some responsibilities!

I came over to the USA, we got married, and within a year I was "hitting bottom." I had never seen so many bars and beer joints, and for me it was like coming to heaven! At the "stag party" before our wedding, I passed out and was put to bed, but I fell out of bed and hit my head on the edge of the radiator. Later, my wife-to-be, her folks, and a couple of other people found me there on the floor. My head was stuck to the floor in my blood, and they did not know if I was "out" because of my drinking or because of the knock on my head. They got me to the hospital, where six stitches were put in my skull, but I did not "come to" until the next morning, wondering why I was in a hospital and what had taken place. I was laughing about this episode, but my in-laws were serious about it. They did not like what they saw happening when I drank.

Since beer was so easily obtained, I soon was drinking on the job as well, and the paint contractor I was working for gave me warnings which only resulted in my being more careful with my use of alcohol while on the job.

As I continued to drink, my problems became more severe, and I blamed my wife for the financial trouble we were having. The first year we were married, we lived in an apartment building, and I was told by the manager that we would have to move out if I continued to drink and make so much noise in the building and in the parking lot. I had passed out in the car, and my head was leaning on the steering wheel, which, of course, set the horn off, and, until someone came and moved me, the horn was blowing like hell in the parking lot. The second year of our marriage, we lived in the lower part of a duplex. The landlady lived upstairs, and she complained about all the empty beer cans in the garbage can. I thought she was one of those "red-necked Norwegians," because she did not use alcohol in any shape or form, and I wanted to tell her so many times.

When I had my first drunk-driving charge, my father-in-law called me an alcoholic, and I did not speak to him or his wife for six months. After several arrests for public intoxication and DWI charges, I began to notice that we were not invited to anyone's house anymore, not even to my in-laws.

I had my own painting business. I had people working for me too, but they did not get paid every Friday as I had promised. After a week and a half of drinking and not showing up on the job, I was told by the builder I was doing the painting for that he was finished doing business with me. Of course, I had to "celebrate" this occasion and ended up in the "drunk tank" again.

I did not have any friends. The people I knew were drinking buddies whom I knew only by first name. Often I would sit in a beer joint and drink all alone playing "Please Release Me" on the jukebox while I cried and sobbed over my sadness and unjust situation. Nobody cared for me anymore. I was a loner and felt lonely even in a crowded bar. I ended up standing on a streetcorner in downtown Minneapolis, begging for money. Some people looked at me, wrinkled their noses, and walked on. Others would drop a nickel or dime—sometimes even a quarter—in my hand. (I did not know one could get arrested for something like that.)

Underneath the Third Avenue Bridge I got acquainted with a Dane who had been a music professor, but, due to his alcoholism, he had lost family and jobs. He took care of me, simply because I was Norwegian, and he always managed to get hold of something to drink. I did not touch wine, even though there were many chances to drink wine. I have not tasted wine since April 3, 1957, the day before I was discharged from the air force. We had a "party" on the base and drank beer, wine, and liquor. Up to that point I had never been so sick from drinking, and I blamed it on the wine, which I was not accustomed to. That had to be alcoholic insanity! I met this Dane two years after I had sobered up, and he cried like a baby—he was so happy for me. Yet, he himself was still living under the bridge.

On one of my DWIs, I passed out at the wheel; the car jumped the curb and ran smack into a house. The front, from the windshield forward, was inside the living room of this house, and the poor people who lived there were quite shaken up. I don't remember too much because I was in the car, strapped in by my seat belt, which I, for some reason, had put on that night. The police said I would have been pinned on the steering column if I had not used seat belts. The car? I got twenty dollars for it because it had snow tires.

To wake up in the "drunk tank" is not a pleasant experience, but after a few times you get used to it. One time I woke up and found myself soaking wet on my back and rear end, but dry in the front. Checking a little further, I found out that the drunk next to me had urinated in his pants. Since we were so close together, like sardines, I got just as wet as he did. This I often refer to as the most "humiliating" experience I have had. I had wet my own pants many times, but being "pissed" on by someone else was much worse, in my opinion. I crawled over to the bowl in the corner to throw up, but it was plugged up. Too many had been there. Then I tried for the sink, but, as I lifted myself up, I could feel the slimy edges of the sink, and, sure enough, the sink had also been used and was plugged up. Someone's false teeth were lying there smiling at me, too!

One time I was thrown out of a beer joint because I was telling "Polack stories." Three guys took me and threw me out on the sidewalk. I hit my head and passed out. When I came to, I saw a blind man standing there, hitting me with his white cane. Others were kicking my ribs in, stepping on my legs, and I thought, before I passed out again: "Svenn, you're really going to the dogs when a blind man starts hitting you with his cane." Someone took care of me that time, too. I do not know to this day how I ended up in that apartment where I finally woke up, sore and aching all over. The first thing I asked for was a drink, which was readily provided.

Another time I got "knifed." It was not much of a stab, but I bled like hell. If someone hadn't taken that guy away from me, he would probably have killed me. Several guys and gals took me outside of the joint where the fight took place, and they took all my clothes, except my underwear. What they needed my old dirty, stinking clothes and shoes for, I don't know, but I tell you, I felt kind of silly standing on the street corner in my white underpants, which by now were red from the blood running down from the wound in my right side. It must have been quite a sight! Finally, a squad car stopped, and an officer wrapped a blanket around me and took me to the general hospital and then to the "drunk tank." There they gave me a pair of overalls to wear.

I could go on relating stories like these, but they are not important. Some have experienced lots worse things than I, and some were not "that bad." I finally ended up in treatment, against my will, but thank you, God, I have not needed a drink since that day.

MY FIRST AA TALK

That Tuesday night in the last half of January, when I first came to this club, I was really amazed to see all of you nice people, so happy, so cheerful, and joking about drinking. I couldn't believe that you were not old, fat, red-nosed guys that I had pictured for myself—surprised also to see the girls who were there, not knowing who had drinking problems and who hadn't. (I still don't.)

I came in that door, walked over to Charlie by the table here, and told him my name and that I wanted to become a member of this group. He led me over there where the coffee is and introduced me to George and Tom and some others of you, and soon I was sitting there on the sofa with Tom, talking about AA. Tom talked most of the time and kept repeating, "You have to keep an open mind."

It got to be eight o'clock, and we brought the coffee cups over to the table, and the meeting started. I was feeling pretty stupid when we stood up, and the rest said "The Serenity Prayer," and I did not know what it was. During the meeting I looked at "The Prayer" and the "Twelve Steps" on the wall and could not get anything out of them. "You're a fool, a big, stupid, Norwegian fool," I said to myself. It was even worse, when the meeting was to close with "The Lord's Prayer." It might seem strange to you, but I could not say "The Lord's Prayer" in English then. I was ashamed of myself. After the meeting, it was more coffee, more talking with Tom, and more of his "keep an open mind." I did not understand what he meant with this saying, but I thought about it afterward. When I came home after that meeting, I was filled with excitement and eager to stop drinking the AA way, as I told my wife.

Three months ago today was Valentine's Day. That's my Dry Date, and I woke up under the Big Clock* downtown. When my brain started to work a little, my first thought was my wife. I was sure that this time she would not put up with me. I had promised so many, many times that I would quit drinking, and I had given her hope now that I had started to go to AA meetings. I saw in my mind how it would be: She, moving to her folks' and I—well, I was not sure what would happen to me. If I had given her a dollar every time I promised her this time would be the last, we would have been debt-free now. My second thought was AA, and this group. I had gotten to know you by name—almost every one of you—and I liked everyone. I felt I had let you all down. A special thought was circling around in my head, and that was what Tom would say. He had talked so much to me and spent a lot of time with me. Now I had the feeling that I had failed.

What would they say at the next meeting? Would they say that "they had the feeling all along that I could not make it"? How stupid can you get? I was so wrong about everything.

Sitting in the courtroom, waiting for the judge to appear, I suddenly saw Ann, her father, and a stranger come in and sit down. I had already made up my mind that I would be sent to the workhouse for quite some time, since this was another drunk-driving charge. I had been in the same courtroom many times before. When I now saw Ann in the courtroom with a stranger, as well as her father, I was convinced that she was going to leave me. That stranger had to be a lawyer. Standing in front of the judge, I could hardly talk. My throat was dry from drinking, and now it was becoming worse from the thoughts I had and the looks of the judge. A rock as big as half the northern part of Norway fell from my heart when the judge said: "One hundred dollars or thirty days." Phew!! I wiped my forehead as I was sent out to the hall. A while later, I was called in to talk to Ann and got to meet "the stranger." It turned out to be a friend of

*The Big Clock is downtown Police Headquarters.

Tom's, another AA man, who started to talk to me about Pioneer House, which I had heard about before—but just the name, not what was going on there.

But I still thought Ann was going to leave me and that this Pioneer House stay for me came in handy for her so she could get things settled in the meantime. After a lot of talk back and forth (but against my inner thoughts), I finally agreed to go to Pioneer House for three weeks. So I left the courthouse with Dick.

I always got drunk at the wrong time. It also seems as if I was testing Ann, testing to see how far I could go before she took action. Now I feel sick inside when I think about the *many* times she had begged me, pleaded with me, cried, and prayed that I would stop drinking. And I promised and promised! As you know, she did not leave me, thank God!

If I had not come to this club when I did, I would never be standing here today talking about this and having these free and happy feelings inside me. I would not have known any one of you, and I would probably still be on the way down the drain.

I have thanked God many times for letting me into this great group. Through the help of you and the AA program, I am proud to say that my life is much lighter for me and my family.

Like so many others, I had a hard time swallowing all the talk about God, this Higher Power. At Pioneer House, there were others with the same feelings as I, but, by talks and discussions, both in classes and at night, I was again and again reminded of Tom's saying: "Keep an open mind." "One day at a time"—"THINK." "Easy does it." Now I know why I saw all these sayings all over Pioneer House the day I came there. They were on ashtrays, on the walls, everywhere!

"God works through people," Tom had said once we were talking, and God sure worked through Tom the three weeks I stayed at Pioneer House. When people you have barely gotten to know take so much interest in you and yours, it must mean that these people have hope for you and that you yourself should start thinking. You feel so tiny and little at the time because you're only receiving and not giving anything in return. But, as time goes by, "one day at a time," you learn that by giving you can also receive.

When it became clear to me that I was an alcoholic and that alcoholism could be arrested, not cured by myself, it seemed easier—easier because I did not have to have any operation. If I had any other sickness, I would like to get well; so, why should I not try to get well in this case, when it did not cost me anything, moneywise. I know that I am a sick man and I also know *what* is causing me the trouble, so it all becomes easier. Just stay away from any beer or booze and I get healthier. It does not cost me money! *It saves me money!*

The Twelve Steps suggested for us on our way to recovery are all in past tense. And, since these steps have worked for others, why shouldn't they work for me? Even in "The Lord's Prayer" we ask for something just for one day: "Give us this day our daily bread." So I ask God to help me stay sober for just *one day at a time.* It's easier that way.

As of today, the first and second steps mean more to me, but I have heard it said by other alcoholics that all twelve are equally as important. Of course, they are, but I talk about my own feelings, and these three months I have been sober I must say that Steps One and Two are the ones that I sort of concentrate on.

He—God—as I understand Him, has got me back to sanity now, and, as long as I continue to practice the AA philosophy, I'll have the best chances ever for a lasting recovery.

The meetings here mean a lot to me. I get something out of every meeting—something to think about for days afterward. If I don't understand something right when it is said, I'll understand it sometime two days later.

I discuss drinking and AA with the guys at work. They are all drinking, more or less, but are pleased that I have found out that I cannot touch it without getting drunk. My boss told me that the other guys had told him that they liked to work with me when I was sober, but when I had been drinking I was an S.O.B.

Today I have been dry for three months—the three happiest months I have had for many years. My wife knows I'll be home from work without stopping at any beer joints or bars, and I feel kind of proud to show her, too, that *I can be trusted.*

Now I can dare to answer the phone when it rings. I also open the door when someone comes and I dare to look people in the eye. Of course, I have not gotten all my bills paid yet, but we're working on them, and one day there will be money for saving, too.

Ford has a commercial about "seeing the light." I feel as if I have seen the light and hope that this light will stay with me forever. It is nice to wake up in the morning and go to work without a hangover!

Now I can smell it right away if someone has been drinking. Now I know how I smelled when I thought I was fooling everybody else.

I believe in God, and, even if I'm not perfect, I'm sure He will take care of me the way *He wants to, not* the way I want to. Since I showed myself and everybody else that I was a poor manager of my life, I accepted that I needed help from God, as I understand him. *He got me back to SANITY,* so I feel quite safe to turn the steering wheel over to Him, and He knows the road I am going to travel anyway.

My prayers might be clumsy, and sometimes I'm hard up for words, but I feel that He will accept them anyway. I thank God for my wife. I thank Him for bringing sanity into my head again so I can enjoy the fellowship here at the group.

I think there are two kinds of friends. Those you spell with a small *f* and those you refer to with a capital *F.* When I talk about you, I always use a capital *F.*

I thank all of you, fellow alcoholics and your spouses, for helping me to keep sobriety. Now my life is worth living again.

MY SECOND AA TALK

The three first words, *CAME TO BELIEVE,* tell us that it is a gradual process. Marvin S. told me something he heard once, years ago. He said:

FIRST; WE *CAME*
SECOND; WE *CAME TO*
Then; WE *CAME TO BELIEVE.*

This makes sense to me, and, the more you think about it, the easier it is to understand. I am very grateful to my sponsor for repeating so many times to me, "Keep an open mind." I think that it helps me very much. I should say that *I know* it helps me. By keeping an open mind, sooner or later it will hit you. Maybe not as a flashing light but you'll understand that all these nice men and women with years of sobriety did not find this happiness in life without help and *faith* in a Higher Power.

Last Saturday night at the Squad 5 meeting, one of the speakers said something that really struck me. He said: "AA is not for those who *need* it, but for those who *want* it." How true that is. It does not help a bit to come in here under pressure from wife or someone else. That way we would not stay sober. If we want AA ourselves, *then* it is always here to help. But AA cannot do everything! We have to do it ourselves by the help of our *Faith* and *Trust* in a Higher Power. AA will supply the materials. *We* have to do the work.

I know, for sure, that it helps me to stay sober by praying for help when I need it and also saying thanks to God for help received. I have a great trust in God. Those who pray to God for help will also receive help.

As we attempt to apply all of the Twelve Steps, we find that they call for the exercise of true humility. This word "humility" gives a new man in AA trouble off and on.

But in order to be humble, we don't have to let the rest of the world walk over us. It simply means a total lack of boasting, pride, conceit, and arrogance. This way you can get a true picture of yourself and your *strengths* and *limitations.* They say that only a *free man* can be humble. If an AA man starts to feel that *he himself* is responsible for his sobriety and success, that man has got his false pride and arrogance back, and at the same time his spiritual strength weakens and maybe disappears, and soon that man is worse off than he ever was. If you want to stay sober and stay happy, always keep in mind that this newfound happiness is directly related to your *Faith* in a Higher Power.

The last part of Step Two says "restore us to sanity." What does that mean? I thought I was as sane as I am today. I just got drunk and could not do things right because of the booze.

My very good counselor at Pioneer House talked to me about this step, and, after we had discussed the many strange things that had happened when I was drunk, he made it clear to me that I *could not* have been sane while I did them. I can ask every one of you here tonight, *"If a movie camera with soundtrack had followed you on one of your 'spinning days,' and you later saw the movie, wouldn't you also doubt your sanity?"* Holy smoke, I believe I did things that even Charlie Chaplin could never do. I know I did things I would not dare do when sober. We have all done both comic and tragic things while we were temporarily insane.

Just think about all the crimes that are committed by people while under the influence of alcohol. Our jails are filled up every day by men and women who, while drunk, did things that they would not dare do without the touch of liquor. They might have thought about them when sober but wouldn't have dared put their plans into action before they had some booze inside to give them courage.

> Insanity, as viewed by the courts, is a term applied to a serious mental derangement or disorder. An insane person

can be dangerous to himself and others. He has a lack of capacity to manage the ordinary affairs of life.

What part of the insane person's body is sick? The *brain.* What part of a person's body does alcohol tend to disintegrate first and most? The *brain.* Our mental hospitals have thousands of insane alcoholics. If they had known how to arrest the disease of alcoholism, some of them would be sitting here with us tonight.

"Came to believe that a Power greater than ourselves could restore us to sanity." Nowhere under the sun is there a breed of men and women in such desperate need of God as we alcoholics. No single group in the entire world is more in need of divine guidance and peace than those who have given up the bottle and are starting out a new way of living. There can be no better safeguard to sobriety than *Faith and Trust in God.* The Twelve Steps are steep and hard to climb, but, as we make the climb, it goes easier when we remember the two handrails we have to hang on to: *God and the AA Fellowship.* It always seems strange when a man who gets into AA discovers the *friendship* we have—*friends we never knew we had.*

History tells us about people from the very beginning who had *Faith* in something. *The Sun* was the strongest thing for Persians and Egyptians, and, therefore, they worshipped the Sun. The early Greeks had plenty of gods, and even the *NORSEMEN* had their *Odin* and *Thor.* We know that wars have been fought because of differences of belief in a Higher Power. Even in darkest Africa, you will find a tribe that believes in something greater than themselves. It might be a mountain or a river or a tree.

I call my Power God. But in AA it is up to each one of us what we will call our Power. It is *God as we understand Him.*

If a cancer patient could arrest his disease, don't you think he would spend days working on it until he found the truth? We all have the same desire to live, and, by a simple "came-to-believe attitude," we can prevent these recurrent fits of insane drunkenness. If you can avoid getting put away in a place for insane persons, if you still want to live, isn't it well worth it to seek help from a Power greater than yourself?

The AA program is one of action. You cannot sit still and expect things to happen. We have to get up and get out and spread the word. From others' experiences I have learned how they work the program, learned about their *Faith in God.* When I see the results, I cannot doubt that our program works.

We have to recognize how strong the Higher Power is, compared to our willpower. Think about the times when you tried to stay sober by yourself. I bet we all tried, but failed. In my case, I did not try to stay sober for Svenn and for Svenn alone, but for my wife, my in-laws, my boss, my neighbors, and so on. It did not work. Now, I stay sober for myself first, and now I also have a faith in God, that I did not have before, and that sure helps me.

A new man will probably say, "What has all this Higher Power got to do with my staying dry? All I want is to get the booze out of my life." I will say it this way:

You can stay sober and dry the rest of your life by cold-blooded murder. You'll be put away and stay sober—but not happy!

You can cross the street when you see a beer joint or a liquor place or even live like a hermit. Whatever you choose, you'll be hard to live with. You would be thinking about all these sacrifices you are making—what a martyr you have become, but happy? NO, SIR!!! Unless happiness accompanies sobriety, your period of sobriety will be short. We all are entitled to happiness but remember: so are those you live with!!

For the new man in the AA program, I'll say that even if your understanding of a Higher Power is kind of weak at this point, just look around you; believe me, it was not easy for *everyone* in this room!

By keeping an open mind, by exposing ourselves to the teachings of other successful men and women, by watching the spiritual growth in others, *we* will gradually "come to believe in a Power greater than ourselves."

Don't be afraid to get on your knees to get on your feet.

SOBRIETY COMES FIRST

When I became an alcoholic, there was nothing I could do about it. The sickness I had gotten made me allergic to alcohol in any form. I am powerless over alcohol, and, when I am powerless over something, then I might just as well give up, because the word *powerless* means exactly what it says.

No doctor or medicine, as of today, can ever make me drink like a social drinker. I am forever powerless over alcohol, and this is what I have to tell myself.

I believe I am powerless over alcohol. I have told myself this for a long time, and I do not want to drink any more than I want *two left feet.* I had my chance to drink socially but I blew it by overdoing my drinking, so I started into alcoholic drinking and became an alcoholic.

I am glad I found out what was wrong with me, before it was too late! I am a sick person!! I have the disease of alcoholism, and the only treatment that works, in my opinion, is a fellowship like AA.

Of course, I tried to stay sober by myself, but somehow it didn't work. Strange as it may seem, the fellowship of AA *does* work for me as it does for thousands of others.

What made me come to AA? Well, I was *sick and tired of being sick and tired.* I was tired of running away from home in the morning before my wife got up to start telling me what kind of guy I was. I was sick of being looked upon as a louse, of walking into my favorite drinking places and feeling everyone say, "Oh, no! Here comes that Norwegian again." Sick of being turned down when I wanted to talk to someone at the bar. Sick of having the drinks spilled on the bar. Sick of hearing the bartender yell at me for using dirty language. I was sick of living like that and I wanted to do something about it.

"The only requirement for membership in AA is a desire to stop drinking." Most of us tried to control our drinking, but right there and then we had *already lost* control. A man who does *not* think he has a problem never tries to control his drinking.

You know, when I was new in AA, I thought that everyone in AA would like to start drinking like a social drinker again, *IF* a pill or medicine were found to make him that way again. I was surprised to find out that the older members would *not* like to go back to drinking again, *NOT even socially!* Now I must say I feel the same way. What I have learned through the teachings in AA has changed my viewpoints a great deal. I like the way I can live now. I do not wish to change it.

The so-called old timers that we have at every squad or group can tell us newcomers what to do and what not to do, and, if we want sobriety more than anything else, we should listen to them. They have been through what we are going through. They know the answer to better living.

"Don't get hungry and tired," was one of the things that I was told. "Stick with the winners," is another one. Those who are on the program are the best ones to show others how to do it. Of course, the first thing we are after when we get into AA is sobriety, but AA is not only that. AA is a way of living, and for many it is hard to accept this new life. We have to surrender to Step One. If we try to fool someone, we are fooling ourselves. Those that have lost almost everything due to drinking and really want to quit surrender and give up. There is no sense in fighting AA. We don't push it on anyone. We have to be asked for help. Then we gladly give of our time to help someone who *has had it*. We are helping ourselves this way, and we can honestly say: "There but for the grace of God."

Relapses occur in every squad or group but they are not necessary! A man or woman with less than three months of sobriety goes back to drinking. That does not surprise me because he did not want sobriety badly enough. But, when someone with years of sobriety starts fooling around and has a relapse, then it hurts. I like to think that when I was sober for one year, my chances for continued, complete sobriety were better than before.

Of course, I have never said that "I will never drink again," because I live this program only twenty-four hours at the time. Staying sober for twenty-four hours is much easier than doing it by the week or month. The program is a continuous striving for improvements. We cannot have any rest periods; but work at it all the time.

They say that our program is not to be measured in years because an alcoholic never fully reaches his goals, and he can never be cured. We have *arrested* our disease so it does not spread.

Life is all a preparation for something better to come. God has a plan for our lives, and it will work out if we try to do *His will for us.* Only God knows what lies ahead for us. He planned it for us.

If someone asks you if AA really works, ask him if the Pope is Catholic. One question is as stupid as the other. We have over eight hundred thousand living, walking, talking testimonials that it *does* work.

As alcoholics, we should never forget *Step Number One.* It is so easy to say that we have taken Step One, *but in my opinion,* it is not enough to admit we are powerless over alcohol. *We have to surrender,* for the simple reason that we do not drink like social drinkers. We have to surrender, not only in our heads, but our *guts* have to know it, too!!

They say that the first three months are the roughest, but for some it might be rough for a whole year or better. Our background does not matter when we come into AA. We are here because we have one problem in common. We are powerless over alcohol, and we have made a mess out of life for ourselves and others. The only requirement for membership in AA is a desire to stop drinking.

If one of you is here tonight for the first or second or third time, let me tell you something you can think about. *If you have given as much as thirty seconds' thought to whether you have a drinking problem or not: YOU HAVE A PROBLEM! If you have tried to control your drinking: YOU HAVE ALREADY LOST CONTROL."*

I tried to switch to beer only, but I still got drunk. Then I tried to stick with vodka only (because vodka doesn't smell), but I still got drunk and I smelled just as bad.

A lot of people think that they cannot be alcoholic because they have not reached bottom yet. Let me advise you that you don't have to end up on skid row before you finally want to do something about your drinking problem. I am not proud of my past, and, if I can help someone in AA *before* he gets down to where I was, I am glad. I have not been as far down as others, but yet there are many who stopped before they came down to my level.

I remind myself about what did happen when I drank, and then I became very grateful for what has happened since I sobered up. When I compare my past with my present, the choice is easy.

I have seen people who have what we know as *"wet brain."* Through drinking, in many cases without seeking help in time, these men and women continued to drink until they were beyond the point where they could be helped. Now they are existing, but *that's all!!!* They don't know time, place, names; they cannot feed themselves, they have to wear diapers and cannot tie their own shoelaces. *There but for the Grace of God—I was helped in time.*

We are very fortunate—we who have given up the booze for a new way of life. We can again live as human beings are supposed to and have the peace of mind that is ours.

Everything depends upon my sobriety. Without it, I am nothing. My sobriety has to come first. I have to stay sober for myself, not for my wife and family, boss, or anyone else.

I almost lost everything while drinking, and I think I *would* lose it if I went back to my former way of living. We are sick people but we also make nervous wrecks out of those we love so much. They are just as sick as we are, and even then they do not have our disease. They have to learn how to live with us, drunk or sober. Thanks to Al-Anon and Alateen this is now possible.

You've all heard that we are supposed to call our sponsor

before we take that first drink, *not after*. But very few do this. When stinky thinking comes to your mind, and that can happen to any one of us, talk to someone in your squad; call someone on the phone. Do not let this go unattended for a long time. Go to *more than* your regular meetings, do things you don't usually do, visit other members. You have got to want sobriety, *more than anything else!* We do care about each other in AA and whether we stay sober year in and year out. We care.

There is only one drink between sobriety and drunkenness!

Don't miss meetings. Our squad meetings are very important to us. It's like making a deposit in a bank, and the dividends are paid daily if we are trying to live this program. If one meeting is not enough for you, visit other squads or groups. I am at our club three or four times every week, guest-speaking at other clubs, visiting other clubs. I am busy with AA, active in AA, and I stay sober, and *I know I am no longer alone.* But it is not enough to stay sober. It is not enough to come to the meetings. We have to try to practice the program in our daily lives to get some results. The dividends!

My own opinion about a slip or relapse is this: The person has not:

No. 1. "accepted and surrendered to step one";
No. 2. "been practicing the program and most likely has missed meetings."

Maybe you are thinking about the holidays ahead. How can I get through Christmas and New Year's without a relapse? My advice would be this: "Continue to tell yourself that you have a sickness which makes you allergic to alcohol. Say it over and over again." If you feel uncertain and restless, make sure you are around other AA members; get to a meeting. There is always a meeting somewhere in your neighborhood—suburbs or towns. Christmas or New Year's, the meetings must go on!

We do care about you! We have been through what you are going through right now. We know what we are talking about.

This is a very simple program to follow. I can do it, and so can you, if you hang around long enough to give it a chance! A relapse or slip cannot be blamed on anyone else but yourself. No one broke your arm or held your mouth open. You did it all by yourself. Whatever reason you think you have for taking a drink, it's just another excuse.

Believe me, *nothing is so bad that a drink can't make it worse!* We might get the idea that we can handle it again but that is just an idea. Once an alcoholic, always an alcoholic. A woman cannot be just a little bit pregnant, and we cannot be just a little bit alcoholic.

"Stick with the winners!" Those who are on the program can tell you and show you that it works, but you have to give it a chance. Do not try to pick the steps apart to fit you better. Too many have tried, only to end up drunk. *I believe* that everything in the Twelve Steps was put there because the founders knew what it would take to make it work. When this program has worked for so many thousands of people, why not then also for you and me?

I live for only twenty-four hours at a time. That's what others try to do, and they are successful and so can I be. But also, I would like to say that, without my Faith in my Higher Power, I would not be sober today! Don't be afraid to get on your knees to get on your feet.

STEP ONE

There really are no shortcuts to Alcoholics Anonymous. Many of us have tried in different ways to find loopholes, so we did not have to do "too much"; but we all found out that in order to gain anything from the AA program, *we had to become as honest as we were capable of becoming.* For most of us, honesty is difficult, while drinking. Once a person has become a pathological drinker, he can never again become a so-called social drinker.

There are only *two alternatives left* for us, either complete *abstinence; or continuation of drinking, knowing that with chronic alcoholism we also will have to take all the pain and sufferings.*

We are past the point where we have a choice. In order to be on the right track from the start, three points are necessary in order to gain the most from our "tryouts" or attempts to recover from alcoholism. First, *honesty.* I need to be as honest as I am capable of being at the time. Second, *openmindedness*—that I keep an open mind about what I hear and see and read. Third, *willingness,* to change and to learn.

Alcoholism and alcoholics are nothing new. Only God knows how many thousands of years intoxicating drinks have been consumed. But it's only since the late 1940s that alcoholism has been treated as an illness by physicians.

AA came about through two professional people's efforts to stop drinking. After many, many failures, they finally discovered that they could remain sober through helping others with a drinking problem. That was in June, 1935. *The Tenth of June, 1935,* is referred to as AA's birthday, because that is when Dr. Bob had his last drink. But, it was not *until 1939 that the* "program" these first few had tried to follow, became a *book, which is called Alcoholics Anonymous.* We refer to this book as "the Big Book," and, if we read the bottom line on the front cover, it states: *"THE BASIC TEXTBOOK FOR ALCOHOLICS ANONYMOUS."*

There are many books written about alcoholism and other drug dependencies, but there is only one book that has the answers: "The Big Book." We are advised to *read, reread and study* this book because all the answers are there, yet I am amazed at how often I hear the AAs state that they have not read it or they don't own a Big Book or that they don't need to read it to stay sober. I say again: no other book has been written that describes for us how to recover from alcoholism! The fifth chapter starts with: *"Rarely have we seen a person fail who has thoroughly followed our path."* It states, to me, that if I follow this suggested recovery program, my chances are very high of "making it." "Rarely," it says, meaning *it happens very seldom that someone returns to drinking while faithfully trying to live the program.*

Let us remember that in the beginning there were only two alcoholics who had attempted to stay sober *by themselves, but they failed to have any success! Together they remained sober,* and from there they went on to help many more. I will quote from the *FOREWORD TO THE FIRST EDITION, as it appeared in the first printing in 1939: "WE, of Alcoholics Anonymous, are more than one hundred men and women who have recovered from a seemingly hopeless state of mind and body. To show other alcoholics precisely how we have recovered is the main purpose of this book."* On page 59 of the Big Book, second edition, it says: "Here are the steps WE took, which are suggested as a program of recovery." Then it goes on, Steps One through Twelve. *We have here a guaranteed program for recovery; yet so many refuse to accept the fact that they need such a program.*

Most alcoholics experience having to make excuses about why they drink, but at the time these excuses are named *"reasons,"* which we have many of. We *escape* reality through the bottle. We feel *maladjusted* to life as a whole. We use alcohol as *medication,* like *sleeping pills.* This type of list could go on and on.

Step One reads, *"We admitted we were powerless over alcohol—that our lives had become unmanageable."*

To admit to someone else that we have a drinking problem is not that easy. I believe that most of us knew that our use of alcohol was *different* from our friends' and neighbors'. *We tried to correct it somehow, but failed,* and when it came to us that we could not do anything about it, we became panic-stricken. Some took the pledge with their clergyman; others gave up drinking for Lent; others for their family or jobs.

Somehow, we knew that continued use of alcohol would ruin us, but we could not help ourselves. There were occasions when I would make the remark to my wife, that "I drink because I am an alcoholic," but it was said as an excuse; not because I believed it. I used this phrase in an attempt to cushion her anger and resentment toward my behavior.

In this world, there are so many things I am powerless over. As an example, I can mention the weather, which I cannot change no matter how much I want to or try. I am powerless over death. People close to me die no matter how hard I pray or how much I want them to continue to live. I am powerless over YOU. I cannot change another human being, *only* myself. I might not like what you are doing, your behavior, but I cannot stop you or change you. Watching any sport on TV, I find myself saying (to the player on the screen) how he should do it, and I often burst out laughing at myself about the insanity of the situation: "talking to the TV."

Being powerless means, in my opinion, that I can *no longer control;* that the person, situation, the weather—whatever it might be—has *more power* than I can come up with. "Powerless over alcohol," we have become slaves to a liquid that changes our feelings, a liquid that has been known to man for hundreds of years, in one form or another. The bottle that used to give us hope, peace of mind, brighter outlook on life, make us happy, ease any kind of problems—*all of a sudden,* it seems as if *this bottle has turned against us! We begin to see the problems we end up with when we drink. We also see that other problems do not go away when we drink.* We accumulate more and more problems. We need to drink because of that, and the rat race is on!

More problems, more drinking, and we continue for a while to try to outrun the problem, but find ourselves exhausted, physically, mentally, and spiritually. Alcohol becomes more important to us than our hobbies, more important than our friends, more important than our families. *The last thing that an alcoholic seems to lose is his job.* The family might be starving and without clothes, but he does not see that. His mind is not able to comprehend what's going on. He keeps on trying to do his job at his place of employment. He needs that check for more alcohol.

When the bottom falls out, *and it will, eventually,* we are dealing with a very sick person, who needs to be nourished back to life in short, safe steps. The alcoholic has to come to a point where he can, with as much honesty as he can muster, say to himself and others, *that he is powerless over alcohol, that he's licked, that he no longer has any control over how much he drinks, how often, with whom, and that he cannot predict his behavior once he begins to drink, that he is completely powerless.*

I believe that an alcoholic needs to look at the past, what has taken place, what problems have developed due to his use of alcohol, before he can truly see how powerless he has become. *It takes a great guy or gal* to admit to being powerless. We are not weak. *I feel the weakness is to let the drinking problem continue without doing something about it.*

Our character defect of Pride plays a huge role during this period of an alcoholic's life. *Pride almost forbids us to admit to being licked, being powerless.* Thoughts that go through one's mind are like this: *"What will my family think, what will my friends say, how can I explain this to my boss and co-workers?"* Actually, most likely *everyone else knows* of our drinking problem, but has not risked talking to us about it. *The alcoholic seems to be the last one to know about his problem.*

It is as if a big burden is taken off our shoulders when we finally can stand up and say that we are powerless over alcohol. At last it's out in the open. I no longer need to hide this from others. I can breathe freely and without fear of being found out.

Finally, it feels good inside when I can look at you, whoever you are, and say to you that, *"I am powerless over alcohol."*

The next big hurdle to overcome is the last part of the first step: *"that our lives had become unmanageable."* None of us likes to admit being powerless; now we are asked to admit that we cannot manage our own life.

Here again, the alcoholic needs to look back at his past, what has happened to him while drinking. Is he capable of taking care of his duties in the family, job, church, community at large? Has it not been difficult to handle daily routines in the past? Alcoholics drink to *escape responsibilities,* and, through *honest search of ourselves,* looking back, we will see that there are very few things we have been able to handle.

Communication with other people has been shut down, at least *"fenced out."* Our self-respect has suffered. Our guilt and remorse feelings have been haunting us for quite some time. How about the financial end? Have I spent money foolishly, even spent money I did not have, or could not afford to spend? Am I able to express myself in regard to feelings I have? I believe that these and many more questions will be answered with a *NO.* My personal opinion of unmanageable is that my *life was, still is, and forever will be unmanageable.* This is how I see it: *When I wake up in the morning, I ask God, as I understand Him, for help and guidance for today. I thank Him for having granted me another day to be alive and ask His help to make the best of it.* During the hours I am awake, I try to live the AA program as best I can, and at night I say thanks to God for the day that has come to an end.

I also need to associate with other alcoholics. I need to share of myself. I need feedback from others, and this I receive from active AA involvement. I need my AA group.

I ask myself, can I claim to manage my own life, when I so desperately need to rely upon God, the AA program, and other alcoholics, in order to remain sober, in order to stay alive? *The answer I give is a big NO!* I cannot claim to be the manager anymore. I had my chance but I blew it. I screwed up and lost my "manager job." I now have to rely on God's guidance every day, practice of the AA program every day, and association with my AA friends on a regular basis.

When we think about having a drink, we are thinking of the kicks we got out of drinking, the pleasure, the escape from boredom, the feeling of being high. What we do not think about is the letdown feeling, the hangovers, the remorse, the money, and all those *ishy* things we had to face the next day. In other words, we are thinking about the assets, not about the liabilities of drinking. Sure we all had some fun times while drinking, but just remember the next morning and how it was to come out of it.

By drinking, we tried to escape from the world that was bugging us, and for a short time we were convinced that this was the way to live. But, when we got sober, we had more problems than before. Sometimes our drinking created more problems for us, but we always blamed it on something or someone else. Never on the booze. Sometimes we got kicks out of buying drinks for others—thinking we were really big shots. Some of us went to places of ill repute, kind of a lower part of town, just to pretend we were big shots.

Have you ever seen a bar or beer joint in the morning before the cleanup begins? The men's room stinks worse than the city dump. Some did not make it as far as the bathroom, and behind chairs and under tables you might see what they had consumed the day before. It's sickening. This is far from social drinking. Most of us here in this room have been sick, too. Remember when you did not dare to move a muscle because that might trigger it off. Remember when you were lying on the floor trying to get your thoughts and eyesight together so you could find out which way to crawl to get to the bathroom. Remember when your pants were wet and you didn't know why. Remember the shaky hands, your head feeling as if a sledgehammer had hit it, your mouth as dry as a ball of cotton. And don't forget the remorse, the guilt.

Yes, I know you can remember it all, and if you try to drink again after you leave here or after you have been sober for a while, you will discover that it will all happen again except for one thing. It's going to get worse!

I'm sure some of you, if not all of you, have experienced that there were some times when you did not know what day it was or if it was six o'clock in the morning or six o'clock in the evening—wondering how you got home and wishing that you hadn't drunk that much.

Sick and tired of this make-believe living, you finally decide to do something about it. Doctors treat you. Psychiatrists treat you. But what happens? You go out and get drunk again. Maybe your doctors advise you to seek help from Alcoholics Anonymous. For some reason that no one really can tell, AA works where everything else has failed. But I believe you have to want the help in order to stay sober.

In AA we try to escape from boredom. We replace it with some activity. I believe that those who get bored in AA are the ones who are not happy in their sobriety. They stay dry, not sober. There is a difference.

Through working at the AA program as best we can, we can get our self-respect back. We also can feel the respect that others give us. But we have to keep in mind that we need to be honest with ourselves at all times before we can attempt to be honest with other people.

We remain sober by helping others with the same problem. We try to build them up instead of tearing them down. The false friendship we had at the bar is replaced with true friends in AA. We reach a point in our sobriety when there are mornings we feel like jumping out of bed and just spreading our arms out and crying out how glad we are to be alive.

Now, most likely, you who are listening to this talk, either have the drinking problem yourself or maybe have a drug dependency, or you are close to someone who has this dependency. I have often said to people, "I can't label you 'alcoholic' until I have heard you say it first." All of us get introduced to the AA program either through treatment or by coming to meetings. None of us will ever remain sober if we do not accept and surrender to the first step.

It is not enough to admit that we are powerless over alcohol. We have to mean it, and we have to let our guts know it: that we surrender to the fact that we have a disease named alcoholism, but it can be treated. This surrender is of great importance to us. A disease never gets better unless it is treated, and, through a treatment program or through AA, we are advised how to go about arresting our disease. Nobody has a cure for alcoholism. Neither can we threaten a disease. It doesn't go away. When the pains from drinking outweigh the rewards from drinking, then the time has come to do something about it.

So, we are left with a choice: either to surrender and get well or to continue to drink and take all the pain that comes with it.

After a while in AA, we realize that we can enjoy sober living. We learn to get along with our family and friends and how nice it is to do an honest day's work. Sometimes we wonder how we could have gone on living as we used to.

My opinion is that the thought of taking a drink might come to us every so often in the early times of sobriety, and, because of this, we need to build up a guard around us against such stinky thoughts. I suggest that you keep on repeating to yourself that you cannot handle liquor any more—that you get in trouble when you drink—that alcohol is poison—that alcohol has become your enemy. Alcohol is poison to us. It leads to the death of the alcoholic. It might be a quick death or it might be a slow death.

The first step, as I said before, reads, "We admitted we were powerless over alcohol—that our lives had become unmanageable." Alcohol has poisoned our love for our family. Poisoned our ambition to work. Poisoned our self-respect, and so on—a long list. We need to train ourselves to think of alcohol as poison so we can be ready to fight if temptations should come along.

Over a period of years of drinking, we have proved to ourselves and to others that we cannot stop drinking by ourselves. Our willpower is nothing. We have to turn to someone for help, and, in my opinion, that someone is a Higher Power or God, as we understand Him. It is known that the most successful and happy AA members are those who have turned their wills and their lives over to God, as they understand Him. May I suggest that we begin by turning our drinking problem over to someone else. God, if you choose. We know we cannot handle this problem alone, so we try whatever is suggested to us, if we are sincere about staying sober.

A person really gets on the program when he gets down on his knees and surrenders himself to God, as he understands Him. "Surrender" means to put your life into God's hands. We let Him handle our drinking problems. But we have to make sure that we leave it with Him, because, if we try to take it back to handle it ourselves, we are going to find ourselves in trouble again.

Don't try to get this program in just a couple of weeks. It doesn't work that way. Nobody ever graduates from this program, and nobody ever has it made. No matter how many years they have been sober, they still have to attend the meetings in order to continue this new way of living. We say often, just relax and take it easy. Keep an open mind. Don't judge anything before it has been fully discussed. Don't think that you are different, that the way you drank was not the way we alcoholics drank, that you are maybe not an alcoholic! Let me tell you. You either are an alcoholic or you are not. There are no in-betweens. It's just like a female. She can't be a little bit pregnant. She either is or she isn't. Once an alcoholic, always an alcoholic.

We have used any possible excuse to drink. Now it's time to start finding excuses for not taking that drink. We are dealing with a disease, about which it is written that it's "cunning, baffling, powerful." We are dealing with alcoholism.

I have often heard from people who have had a relapse that, once drinking starts again, they have a tough time stopping—much worse than they had before.

The AA program is very simple. But we have to give up our old ways and start the new.

Please try to believe what is being told to you. We, who are members of the different AA groups, when we talk, we are not representing AA. We can speak only about our own ideas—how *I* see it, in this case. But I believe that what I have to say is worthwhile listening to, because I have been there. I am a recovering alcoholic. I have been through the different stages, and I have also suffered the different pains that most alcoholics do.

I suggest that if you don't think that our program is simple to follow, then maybe by continued use of alcohol, you will get some brain damage; and maybe then it is going to be simple enough. We have to want sobriety more than anything else. My sobriety has to come first—before my spouse, before my children, before parents, before employer. Sobriety has to be number one. That's the only way it's going to work. My whole life depends upon whether I remain sober or not. In the long run, I am the one who is going to benefit the most by remaining sober, and I am also the one who is going to suffer the most if I return to drinking.

I have, again, often heard from people who have had a relapse, that they begin most likely, by sneaking a drink now and then. But it lasts only for a short period of time before they go on a big bender.

It is quite difficult for some people to accept help when it is offered, and, when we deal with alcoholism, we have to be willing to accept help. The AA program will not fail you as long as you follow the suggested Twelve Steps. The program doesn't fail; but we, as human beings, fail.

I say often that we need to grow up again, that we were like children and need to grow up, but this takes time. Remember, we didn't become alcoholics just overnight, so the recovery program is going to take some time. For the rest of my life—now, how long is that? I don't know any other answer than that the rest of my life is today. Today I intend to stay sober, and I believe that every human being can go without a drink for one day and that's all the AA program suggests—just today.

Maybe you have heard the words, "dry drunk." It simply means that the person is just as mean and nasty sober as when he was drinking. His character defects and shortcomings are out in the open, yet, he is not drinking. This dry-drunk syndrome can happen to anyone; but we see it most often with someone who has not really given up, who is not really on the program.

We do not know of anyone who has become an alcoholic who could then return to social drinking. Many, many have tried, and just as many have failed.

I am an alcoholic. To me, it is no longer the drink that I cannot have, but it's the drink that I do not want. I am sober because I choose to be—because I have found a new way of life. We might often say I have another drunk coming, but do I have another recovery coming? I hope to God I never need to find out. As of this moment, there is not that much money available that could get me to take that first drink. I don't know about tomorrow, so that's why I said, *as of this moment,* there is not enough money to get me to take a drink. I want to be around to see my children grow up and to be a help to other alcoholics. I honestly have to say I don't find myself with too much spare time, and, really, the time that we have on earth is so short, now that I have finally been born again, I want to spend my time wisely. I lost so much during my drinking—so much time. Time that I can never regain.

Yesterday is gone, and tomorrow is not here, but today is the most important day in my life. Today is the first day of the rest of my life. Don't be afraid to get on your knees to get on your feet.

STEP TWO

In this chapter I would like to talk about the Second Step of the AA program. Bear in mind that it is the way I see it—the way I understand it—and the way that I try to follow this step.

We have to presume that we have now broken through the First Step, and we have admitted and accepted being powerless over alcohol and that our lives have become unmanageable.

Our Second Step reads, "Came to believe that a power greater than ourselves could restore us to sanity." Many of us alcoholics, when we see this step for the first time, cry out that we are not going to have anything to do with that because we have rejected church and God for quite some time. When we see the words "power greater than ourselves," we immediately refer to a spiritual, or rather religious, part of life, and we want nothing to do with that. I would also like to state loudly and clearly right now that we are not dealing with a religion. We are not dealing with a church nor denomination. We are simply going to talk about one person's relationship to a power greater than himself. I do not care what people call their Higher Power; I just know for me, it is God. I have always referred to God, and I think of Him as being God, up in heaven, the one I, as a child, was brought up to believe in.

Many of us also reject looking at the word "sanity." We deny having been insane. We are not capable of seeing that for part of our lives, during our drinking days, we showed an awful lot of insane behavior.

As I look upon the Second Step it says, "Came to believe . . ." indicating to me that it is something that does take place over a period of time. I have often said that first, we come—first, we arrive—maybe in jail, maybe in a treatment center, we arrive in a detox facility or we arrive at an AA group. But we arrive *someplace.* And after a while, depending upon whether we were drunk or not, we come to find out where we are at, if we are in our home county or if we are even in a different state. But we "come to" long enough to start opening our eyes, opening our ears; and some of us, at least, try to listen to what's being said to us. We don't always believe what is being said. We tend to minimize our drinking and the problems that have come about because of drinking. As time goes by—we are now talking about a few days, maybe a few weeks, maybe even months—we finally come to a point where we start believing that there might be a hope for us, too. There might be light at the end of the tunnel, so to speak.

My personal experience was that I felt hopeless. I felt that there was no way in hell that I could quit drinking. But, after a few days out in that treatment center, I became aware that other people had the same problem as I, and they were trying to do something about it, so I came to believe that there was hope.

I am of the opinion that there is hope for anyone as long as there is life. When we stop taking in polluted air, then we are hopeless in my opinion. I don't care how many times a person has been to a treatment center or how many times he has been in and out of AA. As long as he is alive, there is hope.

There must be a purpose in life for every one of us. We can question until we are blue in the face why these certain things happen to us—why we have to suffer so long. Why we have to go through the hell we go through? But there is a reason. I firmly believe that.

I have often heard it said, in different AA groups, that if you can't believe in God as our Heavenly Father, why not believe in the group, why not believe in the Sun. Believe in something that has more power than you. Well, I have to admit that I have never advised someone to believe in something like that. My personal opinion is that an alcoholic will take any shortcut that he can find. He has been used to that for years and years. So, giving an alcoholic a chance at getting a shortcut is like believing in that group of people or believing in that tree or the river, the mountain, the Sun. To me, that is a shortcut—an easy way out—and I would never advise that. I know from my personal experience that, unless we come around to believing in God as a Supreme Being—something you can't see and touch with your own hands—we are all going to have problems remaining sober. I repeat, it is only a personal opinion.

I also hear it said quite often by people who come into treatment or into AA that they have lost faith—they have no faith. Isn't it remarkable how we all practice faith every day—yes, all of us practice faith—but we don't identify it as faith. For instance, how many of you have gone up to the bus driver and asked for his driver's license? How many of you have questioned a taxicab driver as to whether he had a license to drive the cab or not? And how many of us have checked the airplane pilot? No. I guess you, like me, haven't done this. We accept on faith that whoever is up in front there knows what the heck he's going to do with the steering wheel or the "whatever." We trust; we have faith that he who is up there in front knows what he's going to do. We practice faith when we come into a room and we need to turn the lights on. We touch that switch, and, if the light doesn't come on, we will bitch about it. We expect light, and, when the light comes on, we take it for granted. But have you seen electricity? Well, that's a question I ask often of a patient or a person who claims to have no faith. Have you seen electricity? He'll say yes, of course, see the light! We see the light. We see the outcome of electricity. We see what it produces, but you or I have never seen electricity; we *believe* it's there.

What I had the biggest problem with, when attempting to work at this step while in treatment, was this being restored to sanity. I completely denied having been insane. At the time, the only place I knew of where people who had mental problems were sent, was to St. Peter's State Hospital, and I hadn't been there. I knew I hadn't been there, so I couldn't be insane. I argued with other patients, I argued with my counselor about this for a few days, until finally one day he said, "Have you ever taken a good look at what behavior you were showing at times?" "What behavior," I said. Now, this was a new alley for me. It was a new role. No, I hadn't looked at my behavior. So, when I started to look at my behavior—both while "under the influence" and in between my binges (while I was still going on binges—at the end of my drinking I didn't go on binges; it was a steady drunk). I started to take a look at my behavior, and, believe me, it wasn't pleasant, what I found. The way I had treated myself—the way I had treated those that I love—the way that I had treated people, in general, was not good. I was ashamed. There are things I did while under the influence that I would not do sober. Some of the things I wouldn't have the guts to attempt to do sober. But the insanity of it—how come a person can be fairly decent—I say that again, *"fairly decent,"* when sober and then, when under the influence of alcohol, he turns into a raving maniac. He commits cruelties of all kinds. He commits crimes that he wouldn't think of committing sober. I know that it is not sane behavior to sit behind the steering wheel of a car when you are too drunk to walk. I know it is insane behavior to spend your whole paycheck on a Friday night and Saturday just drinking when there are bills to be paid—when there are financial obligations that we have that need to be handled, and yet I spent a whole paycheck more than once while I was still working. At the end of my drinking, there wasn't enough money to buy food, and my wife had to seek employment in order to eat. That is my statement or my opinion—she had to seek employment so she could eat. The only thing that was left in our refrigerator when I went into treatment was a bottle of ketchup, and it wasn't a full bottle, either. Insane behavior—for a married man to come home at odd hours of the night, very much intoxicated, and demand sexual intercourse with his wife—the same wife he was very mean to that morning, calling her names because she brought up his drinking from the night before—the same wife that is begging, praying, crying to get him to stop drinking—the same wife that he badmouthed at the bar—this is the same wife he tries to have intercourse with when he comes home so drunk that he can hardly find the bedroom, and, when he gets refused, he creates more hell, and, if he doesn't get refused, but is unable to have sexual intercourse, then he is not man enough to take this as his own responsibility, but rather claims that it is her fault.

We are very, very good at finding fault with other people, particularly our wives, or for you female alcoholics, you find fault with your husbands, I'm sure. The insanity of alcoholism, we can read about in the Big Book. Among other things, it says we are dealing with alcohol: "cunning, baffling, powerful."

God, as I understand God, is a loving God. He loves me very much. I believe what the Scriptures say, that he loves me many times more than I love my own kids. Those of you who are parents—think about the love you have for your kids. I have observed when I am away from my kids that I miss them so much at times that it hurts, and then, when I think about God loving me more than that, it is so unbelievable—I can't understand it—that Someone can love me that much.

I am not religious. I go to church, yes; but I am not religious. I know, from my own experience, how important it is to believe in a Supreme Being, I prefer to say God, in order to start this recovery program and make it last.

So, the Second Step says, "Came to believe that a power greater than ourselves could restore us to sanity." It isn't going to happen overnight. It isn't going to happen just because we want it that badly. No, it will happen only when we become as honest as we are capable of becoming and when we become as sincere as we are capable of becoming. When we have been sober for a while, we can start talking about our insane behavior in our AA group or with a few close friends. When we can talk about how insane we behaved at times, then, I feel, we are getting with it—we are getting on the program. When we can laugh at ourselves for the silly things we did and said, when we can laugh even at what we refer to as being the worst things that happened to us, then we are beginning to get well.

Just look around in any AA group. There are old-timers. There are people who have been sober twenty or thirty years. They never got that amount of sobriety overnight—only a day at a time. And you and I are going to obtain sobriety—length of sobriety—a day at a time. No, it can't be given to us. It can't be handed to us on a silver platter. We have to earn it, and we earn sobriety a day at a time by practicing these Twelve Steps that are handed to us as a guideline for recovery. There are hundreds of thousands of men and women who have sobered up and gained a useful purpose in life by attempting to live these steps, so why not you and I? It begins with you and me. It begins with you and me starting to want a change of lifestyle. It begins with our willingness to listen and keeping an open mind so we can become a little more honest a day at a time.

So, in concluding this chapter, I will say the Second Step, "Came to believe that a power greater than ourselves could restore us to sanity," means exactly that. It means that you and I need to work hard. If we continue to work, we are going to go places. If we give up, we have lost. So please, "don't be afraid to get on your knees, to get on your feet."

STEP THREE

In this step one thing is necessary, and that is willingness—willingness to open ourselves up to the fact that we need help from outside. We are no longer able to do this alone. The willingness that is necessary will open the door for any one of us who wants sobriety. We cannot sit on our rear ends and expect things to happen. No sir! We have to get into action.

For many of us, this step probably means that we are going to make a serious decision for the first time in our lives. When I first was introduced to this step, while in treatment, I thought turning my will and my life over to the care of God meant that I had to become a Salvation Army officer. That was my way of thinking of doing God's work, turning my life over to Him, so to speak. I knew the Salvation Army very well, because they had fed me on many occasions when I was still a "bum." It took a while before I could understand what was meant by this step.

My counselor often said that my way of running my life hadn't proven much, and to that I had to agree. It seemed as if when I was doing things my way, most of the time I ended up with manure on my hands. So, little by little, I came to a point that I had to make a decision whether to be serious about quitting drinking or just to hang there, not knowing what to do. When we look at our past, I think that most of us will agree that our way of making decisions, our way of living our lives wasn't exactly what we had set out to do in the beginning. In many cases, we have not lived up to our own expectations of ourselves, and we certainly haven't lived up to other people's expectations either. Making this decision of turning my will over to God means that, as far as I understand, I let decisions be made for me by God, as I understand God. Certainly, I know that God does not come down on earth and say, "Svenn, this is what you are going to do; Svenn, this is what you are not going to do." No, that's not the way it works, but I ask God's help in decision-making. I start my day by asking God for help and guidance for everything that I am going to undertake today. This is the way I start my day. But, I have often said that, by nine o'clock, I need to do this whole thing over again. Sometimes by nine o'clock I have needed to do the Third Step three times, because I find myself wanting to do things my way, and, unless I catch myself doing this, I might end up with manure on my hands again.

Life on earth is very short. Just think about the last ten—twenty—thirty years. How fast they have gone by, and how little we have accomplished. Now we are at the point where a decision needs to be made whether we are going to be serious, sincere, and honest—or if we are just going to play a game because we do not intend to stop drinking at all. In my opinion, here is where the decision needs to be made—whether we are going to drink or not. Because, if we are going to do it our way, we will continue to drink.

Often, I hear it said by people who are either coming into AA or coming into treatment that they have so much willpower. Well, we have shown a lot of willpower, but what has it amounted to? We have had the willpower to continue drinking. Even though we might have gone down the drain, slowly but surely, physically, mentally, spiritually, and financially, we continue to have the willpower to drink. So my constant answer when someone talks about willpower and stopping drinking on willpower is this: "Try willpower next time you have diarrhea. Try willpower next time you have a toothache. Try willpower next time you have a headache, an earache, or when your appendix needs to come out. Whatever illness or pain you have, try your willpower. See how great it is." Believe me, my friend, those of us who have made this turnabout and who have been down the drain have found our way out of there by making use of the AA philosophy. We have tried all those ways and it didn't work. And those who were in the program when we sobered up (the old-timers) have also tried it. I suppose that some people have to try no matter how much they are told it is not going to work; they still have to try. It's almost as if they're all from Missouri—they have to be shown.

Our willpower is so frighteningly weak when you think about the power of God, as we understand God. What can I do if it rains? Can I stop it? No. What can I do to stop that truck or that train or that airplane? Nothing. I am powerless over those things too. And, if it turns out to be 32° on the Fourth of July, can I make it become 90° just by saying, "Let us have 90°?" No. It doesn't work that way. I don't have the power. Someone has that power to determine what temperature we are going to have, whether the sun is going to shine, and also whether the moon is going to shine upon the earth at night.

It takes us a while before we really understand how powerless we humans really are compared to God's power. I was asked by my counselor to try to figure out who would lose on a deal like this. Would I or would God? He said you can think of your weight—the meat, the fat, the bones, and don't forget all the bull-shit, he added—and then compare it. That is what I am going to give God. Now, what am I getting in return? He laid it on the table to me that I could find happiness, serenity, and peace of mind. I could have a useful life ahead of me. I had to admit that I was not the one who would lose in a deal such as this. So, little by little, I started to work at making this decision to turn my will and my life over to the care of God, as I understand Him.

Through the years, I have worked with many, many people, and I have seen, from time to time, that some people (especially men) are somewhat afraid of talking about God or talking about the spiritual part of this program. They might have a good relationship with God of their understanding, but still they have a hard time talking about it in AA meetings.

I am of the opinion that we are not weak. We couldn't help it that alcoholism came into our lives. That we became alcoholic does not mean we are weak, but we still need help to overcome this in order to have a lasting sobriety.

I have no power over my life in that sense that I didn't determine that I was going to be born. Neither am I the one to determine when I am going to die. How often have we heard about alcoholics who tried to commit suicide? But we even louse up that attempt. I was also one of those who wanted to end my life, and on two occasions I tried. But I was drinking, of course, in order to have the guts to go through with it, and, both times, I passed out. There had to be a reason why I survived, why I am still alive. There is a reason why you and I are here on earth. I know that we question from time to time why a young person dies and why an old person, who is praying to die, still is kept alive, even if it is done by machines. But, it is not up to us to understand. If we were meant to be able to understand God's doings, then, he would have made us that way from the very beginning. We are born with a free mind, and, as we grow up, God lets us make decisions; he lets us run our own lives so we can see how we can foul up our own life and other people's lives. God knows that eventually some of us are going to come around and "see the light." But, there are those also who do not "come around." We refer to those people as "wet brains." "Wet brains" are people who, due to abuse of alcohol, no longer have the capacity to think or make decisions. They have to be institutionalized. They have to be fed. Some wear diapers, and it is really sad to visit a state hospital or a Veterans' Administration hospital and see these souls that are now existing, not living (in my opinion). Of course, this can happen to you and me, too, if we continue to drink. So, the founding fathers made this program available for us, so you and I could come around to looking at that Third Step and say, "Yes, I better make a decision before it is too late."

Don't be afraid to talk about your beliefs and your faith. Without them, we are lost. We need to depend upon that power greater than ourselves. We need to depend upon and trust God, as we understand God.

It might look as if this step is almost impossible to follow, but it isn't, not when you think that we have over a million alcoholics who are sober today. Sobered because they try to live this program a day at a time. That is bound to tell me something. Hopefully, it is also telling you something—that this program works when we really want it to.

The Third Step says, "Made a decision to turn our will and our lives over to the care of God, as we understand Him." My will and my life I place in the hands of God every morning. Yet, I need to do it several times every day. It isn't something we do once and are done with forever. No, not at all. We continue to practice every step, no matter how long we stay sober. I have not become religious, but my faith in God has grown stronger and stronger as my sobriety has gone on. I believe that God's will for me is that I, first of all, stay sober, and then that I try to do my best. He is always going to be there to guide me and to help me if I am willing to trust in Him, if I am willing to let Him be by the steering wheel. If I take over the steering wheel, chances are great that we are going to go into the ditch. But, as long as I leave the steering wheel to Him, I am going to go places, and I am going to have a safe trip. That I firmly believe.

I also believe that either we turn around and start believing in the power greater than ourselves and make a decision to turn our will and our life over to God; or we will continue to be hopeless egotists and our chances for recovery are going to be mighty slim.

We have, by now, taken a look at the First Step. We have admitted to our alcohol problem. We have admitted to our unmanageability. In the Second Step, we made efforts to come to believe that there was a Power greater than ourselves that could be of help to us and steer us in the right direction. Now, the Third Step advises us to make a firm decision that this Power greater than ourselves is going to be of help to us if we are willing to let It be so.

It takes practice. It takes repetition after repetition. Nothing good in life comes easily. Sobriety is not going to come easily for everyone, but all of us have to work at it. We have to work at this program to have a lasting sobriety.

I hope that whoever reads this will do some work and will make some effort to find a Power greater than themselves to trust. And I will close with, "Don't be afraid to get on your knees to get on your feet."

STEP FOUR

After having worked through the first three steps of the AA program, we are now faced with the tough undertaking of looking at ourselves as honestly as we can.

In Step One, we admitted to being *powerless over alcohol* (or other drugs). We honestly looked at how our abuse of alcohol had us licked, how weak our willpower really was.

We came around to accepting that our way of drinking was *not social,* that we had become *dependent upon alcohol, "cunning, baffling, powerful."* Tough as it was, we finally gave up the fight and surrendered to our powerlessness. We also had to take a close look at the unmanageable parts of our lives. When we came down to the "nitty gritty," there was really not much left that we could manage.

"That our lives had become unmanageable," it says, and unless we can accept that, we will again try to "manage," and again we will find ourselves with more problems.

In Step Two, we began to see the light—hope—at the end of the tunnel; we could see the "insane behavior" we had shown at times. Hopefully also, finding a *"power greater than ourselves"* has helped restoring us to sanity. *This step indicates that this will take time; we will not achieve anything overnight. A process is taking place, slowly, but surely.*

In the Third Step, it is suggested that we *turn our will and our life over to "God, as we understand Him."* My opinion is that we can begin the Third Step by turning our drinking problem over to our Higher Power, *God,* if you wish. It does state in the Third Step: *"Made a decision to turn our will and our lives over to God as we understood Him."* That means that we have a decision to make, something we cannot "put off" until later.

Keep in mind, we are *never* done working these steps, but it is on a daily basis that we "live the program."

By continued practice of the program, we are guaranteed a happier life.

So, having come this far, we are now going to sit down and write our inventory. Before any of us came into the program, we had been busy, at times, taking everyone's inventory but our own, constantly finding "fault" with other people.

In my opinion, there are three things that our inventory must consist of, namely that it must be:

Honest
Searching
Fearless

Before we even get to the Fourth Step, I feel pretty sure that we have heard a lot about honesty, that, without honesty, we are not going to make it. If we cannot be honest with ourselves, we are not capable of being honest with others. Honesty with ourselves begins at the first step, and it's *the backbone of the AA program.* Continued self-dishonesty will also bring continued drinking after a few days, weeks, months.

For a person like me, who for years had lived on lies, and dishonesty in thoughts and behavior, it does not come easy suddenly to change to a fully honest and open way of living.

Honesty touches every aspect of our lives. In dealings with ourselves and with other people, honesty is a part—a big part—of the relationship.

I often find myself involved in dishonest thinking, and, of course, nobody but me knows about it *except God,* who knows everything.

I am not ashamed of being human, and, because I am human, I have not been able to rid myself *completely* of my character defects.

Maybe because I was so dishonest, so phony in my past, maybe because I disliked myself so much for that phoniness, maybe that is why I have such a hard time tolerating dishonesty and phoniness now, both within myself and other people.

We do not become saints!

In the fifth chapter of the Big Book, it states: *"we claim Spiritual progress, rather than Spiritual perfection."*

My opinion is that I cannot be completely honest, only as honest as I am capable of being at this point. I believe *only God* can be complete in anything.

I am not honest all the time. I speed on the highways, and I have more than once told a person that he was going to survive the "withdrawal pains," even though I did not believe it. Try to understand what I am saying. It is only on a daily basis that we live the program, and one of our AA slogans is "twenty-four hours at a time." Today I am not going to drink. Today I will work on one specific problem I have. Today I will not boast, lie or con anyone. I am not without fear every twenty-four hours that go by. Neither can I say that I am humble every twenty-four hours. I don't pray to *God* every minute for twenty-four hours.

I find myself doing things "my way" several times in one day, and I turn my will and my life over to *God* many times each day. He knows what is happening with me.

Due to our *disease of alcoholism,* our *character defects* have become more frequent in appearance, stronger in duration, and it is no longer a secret to people around us what is going on with us.

We have drifted into wrong actions, wrong attitudes, wrong viewpoints and so on.

In either event, we need to take a close look at ourselves, and the one that is suggested is an *honest inventory. Keep in mind: This inventory is of ourselves, NOT our wives, children, bosses, neighbors, or anyone else. Nobody else but ourselves!*

We search for the truth!

Searching means to me, that I go back as far as I can remember, letting my memory bank replay past happenings, both good and bad. Some people, I have heard said, believe that it is not necessary to look at our lives before we became alcoholics.

In my opinion, I feel we need to take a close look at our past, as far back as we can remember, because we most likely showed dishonesty, for example, long before we became addicted to alcohol. Maybe it was cheating in school, stealing candy at the drugstore, lies that were told. It is far from pleasant to look at our past, since we have tried to cover up the past through our drinking years, not allowing the past to surface. Now that we are going to be honest with ourselves, we write down on paper what we find, and we cannot deny it; we cannot say it is Tom, Dick, and Harry. No, it's nobody else but me, and that hurts!

While I was working on my Fourth Step one evening, my counselor came into my room, and, finding me with tears on my cheek, he said: *"When you hurt in your Fourth Step, you'll have a good Fifth Step, and your chances for 'making it' are higher."* I did not understand what he meant, at that time, but, as time went on, I know that only through an honest inventory will *hurts* come about. Those who only "skim the top" in their Fourth Step are also having problems staying sober.

I am not ashamed or afraid of saying that I cried more than once during my Fourth-Step inventory. It was difficult to believe that this was me, because I had never taken a close look at myself. I did not know I was such an animal! *Hurts and pains seem to be necessary in order for an honest Fourth Step to be completed.*

Every one of us likes to be liked, and we have, at times, played the game of "people-pleasing." We are afraid of letting others know *who* we are because then they might not like us.

Here, in the Fourth-Step inventory, we have to let everything come out, no matter how *"bad"* we believe it is. Holding back is a big risk to take, and, more often than not, those who do return to drinking have been holding back something that should have been brought out in their Fourth Step.

Honesty, first and last—*honesty.*

I don't believe that we are really aware of what we might find in our search for truth. Something will hurt; others will make us feel better about ourselves.

But we cannot afford to be afraid. It states "fearless, moral inventory." Some of the things we have done, we classify as "bad." My point is that we are basically good people, but, because of our alcohol problem, we have shown behavior that is classified "bad." You and I as persons are not "bad." We are not "rotten" all the way through, even though sometimes we feel that way. *"Nothing we have done is so bad that God will not forgive us. God loves you and me; that's why He forgives us."*

What are the things we need to look at? *There are four main things* which we need to examine ourselves in:

A. Personality Defects
B. The Seven Cardinal Sins
C. The Ten Commandments
D. Virtues, Attitudes, Responsibilities

Keep in mind, if we sincerely want to sober up and remain sober, these are the *suggestions* to follow, *which have been proven to have more "success" than anything else that has been tried.*

List of thirteen character defects:

1. Selfishness
2. Alibis
3. Dishonest thinking
4. Pride
5. Resentments
6. Intolerance
7. Impatience
8. Envy
9. Phoniness
10. Procrastination
11. Self-pity
12. Feelings easily hurt
13. Fear

A friend of mine, Father Lugar, who has heard thousands of Fifth Steps, advised the client/patient to make examples (on paper) where he had shown these defects, just so the clergyman could see that the patient knew what each of these defects means.

We have, every one of us, been guilty of showing many of these thirteen character defects; maybe someone has even more than just thirteen.

We need to look at the Seven Cardinal Sins and examine ourselves to find out where we have shown lust, envy, gluttony, and so forth. Nobody knows what has been going on *inside us* better than we do ourselves, and *Honesty* is the key word here.

We need to take a close look at the Ten Commandments, since most of us have been having problems living up to God's Law. We have, at times, taken God's name in vain, rejected His house, denied His existence, and many of us really need to check each and every Commandment.

Since alcohol or other drugs are not going to be part of our lives from now on, we need to place something in its place. Stopping drinking is not enough. That is like putting the cork in the bottle, but not doing any work on ourselves.

What we need most of all are tools to work with. We are in desperate need of Faith, Hope, and Charity. Faith is needed to succeed. We acquire *Faith* through prayer and meditation; *Hope,* for continued lasting sobriety and recovery; *Charity,* showing gratitude to God, as we understand Him.

We also need to build on the good points that we have. Yes, we do have good points, even those of us who thought we were the lowest of everything that was alive. If we were "all bad," nobody would care about us.

Our attitudes can also stand some improvements: attitudes and responsibilities toward God, toward ourselves, our family, our job, our friends, neighbors, and toward AA.

In closing, let me say that the one we end up cheating the most is ourselves, if we try to go easy on ourselves in our inventory. Let us try to be as honest as we are capable of being, because it might be our very last chance at doing something positive for ourselves. So, remember, "Don't be afraid to get on your knees to get on your feet."

STEP FIVE

Having gone through the Fourth-Step inventory where we have written down the character defects that we have, we have dealt with the Ten Commandments and we have dealt with the Seven Cardinal Sins. Now, in this step, we are to sit down with another human being and then talk about ourselves. It is in this step, I believe, that we get to face the facts for sure. For so many years we have covered up and tried to forget certain episodes and certain deals and wrongdoings, but now these things will have to be talked about out loud. Oh, yes, we have known everything, but we have pushed and pushed these thoughts way back into the part of our brain that stores our memory. Part of the guilt of keeping all these things inside, I believe, also refers to our knowing that God knows everything that goes on with us. We have guilt from hiding things from God. We have guilt from hiding things from other people. God has also known about us and everything that we have participated in. We have, in most cases anyway, conveniently neglected openly to ask God for forgiveness, and maybe some of you, like me, also neglected to go to church and maybe resented God for what, in our sick minds, he was doing to us. Now all of this has to come out into the open.

What a torture it is for sick people like us to go through the Fourth and Fifth Steps. I can remember how I tried to look at anything other than the clergyman's eyes while telling him about my past. I had never in my life, up to that point, sat down and told someone about my innermost feelings and my innermost hurts. No one had really heard what Svenn was really like, and, as I sat there with this clergyman, I tried to look everyplace else, but, somehow, there was something with him that drew my eyes back to him. And, somehow, he also got me to say things that I hadn't even thought of. He could ask questions about what I was talking about and thereby open up channels for me so I could deal with other things in regard to what I was talking about. There was something with that person that drew my eyes back to him, and I could in no way escape from telling him exactly what I felt.

I am one to believe very strongly that we need a written Fourth-Step inventory. It hurts so much more to see it in writing than just to think about it. I also believe that, as soon as our Fifth Step is over with, the papers where we wrote out our inventory should be destroyed. In no way do I suggest that anyone keep those papers lying around; yet I have seen people come to treatment and bring with them their Fourth-Step inventory that they took several years ago in another treatment center. In such cases, I ask them to bring this inventory to me, and I will keep it locked up in my desk until they are discharged, and then I advise them to destroy those papers plus the Fourth-Step inventory that they wrote while in treatment. If they are allowed to keep the old inventory, they won't be doing any work on themselves while in treatment this time. And no matter who we are and where we have been, we need to take a new inventory for every new Fifth Step that we are going to have.

One thing is to write out the Fourth-Step inventory, but here in the Fifth Step we are advised to sit down and openly admit, loud and clear, to God, to ourselves, and to another human being the exact wrongs that we have committed.

I tend to believe that some experience, some awakening, took place with me when I had my first Fifth Step. As I said earlier, I had never sat down to tell anyone what I was really like. I had, of course, written out the Fourth-Step inventory, and I had gone through all kinds of hell while working on my Fourth Step. So there was a change that was taking place with me as I went into this Fifth Step with this clergyman whom I had never seen before. I tend to believe that a spiritual awareness, awakening, experience—I don't know what word to use, but *something* happened to my spiritual beliefs. I have heard this said by many people that, after their Fifth Step, it's as if a ton is lifted off their shoulders—that they have gotten rid of the garbage, and they can breathe more freely.

I also believe that we should be careful whom we choose to have our Fifth Step with. Now I know that in the early days of AA, there were no trained clergy to have Fifth Steps with. The members used their sponsors. They used lawyers. They used doctors. Nowadays, we are so much more advanced, I daresay. We have trained clergy that will hear our Fifth Steps, and they can help us so much more because they have training in this field. There are many, many trained clergymen throughout the United States.

The longer we procrastinate doing the Fourth and the Fifth Steps, the longer time we wait, the harder it's going to be to get going. Every human being has character defects, but I also know that we alcoholics tend to show our defects so much more, particularly, while under the influence.

Due to my illness of alcoholism, some of my defects were "turned on," so to speak, and everyone around me became aware of these defects. When I in turn found out that others knew about me, I drank more to escape that torture. Whether I drink or not, my defects are still with me; but I am now more capable of controlling some of these defects. For example, I do not have to lie anymore. I don't have to come up with alibis, and I can look people straight in the eye. I can give compliments and mean them, where, in the past, it was just for one reason that I gave compliments—because I was looking for something. For me it was lying that was my biggest defect. I don't believe, as I said, that we ever get rid of all our defects. There are many times that I find myself wanting to tell a white lie. There is no such thing as a white lie. Either we lie or we tell the truth. Yes, I have every defect that I used to have, and I need to work at these defects to keep them down; I pick certain defects to work on today, to try to improve, but I still get angry. I get hurt and I get resentful, and I can go down the whole list of defects. But I also do know that I have a choice now. I can choose if I want to feel this way or that way. I didn't have a choice before; but, since I came into the program, this choice has been made available for me. Having gone through what we have gone through, it is a great adventure to get release from these guilts and hurts that have been with us for years and years.

The AA program promises us a new way of life, and I personally do not believe that I could have found what I have found if I had not become an alcoholic and been introduced to the AA program.

There has to be a change that takes place with us—both inside and also around us. I can still hear those words that my counselor told me when I was in treatment. He said if you don't hurt in the Fourth and Fifth Steps, you haven't done much of a job; but, if you hurt while doing these two steps, your chances are a lot higher for recovery. At the time it was said, I didn't understand it, but after I had been sober awhile, I understood what he meant, and now I use the same suggestions for other people.

Now, the program suggests that we live every step, from one to twelve, yet I know that there are many who procrastinate, many who suffer for a long time before they finally get around to having a Fifth Step. But, after they have had their Fourth and Fifth Steps, it is also noticed, the change takes place with them. I believe very much that every step has to be lived, but I also know that some steps are more important to me today. I need to work harder at some steps today than yesterday or maybe tomorrow.

Our Fourth-Step inventory has to be as honest as we are capable of making it in order for us to have an honest, good Fifth Step. If we cheat ourselves in these two steps, we will eventually be drinking again. As I have said before many, many times, this program demands H-O-W: Honesty, Openmindedness, and Willingness. We admit to God. We finally admit to ourselves, and now to another human being the exact nature of our wrongs. But also keep in mind; we haven't been all bad. There have to be some good points that we need to talk about. I know, for instance, in my own case, I am a housepainter by trade, and I know I did a good job when I was sober, and I still have some letters of reference from some well-to-do people that I painted for, so I know I did a good job. My counselor advised me to put that down in my Fourth-Step inventory. At least there was one thing good. I was also kind to my cats. I had never abused the cats. These things seemed so unreal at the time, but he was trying to open the door for me so I could understand that I hadn't been all bad. It's easy to find fault with ourselves, but we also need to look at the other side—there are some good things, too.

Let us be as honest as we are capable of being, because we are the ones who are going to benefit the most for being honest, and, as usual, I will end with "Don't be afraid to get on your knees, to get on your feet."

STEP SIX

If we have been as honest as we are capable of being in the Fourth-Step inventory, I believe we have come to realize how many glaring defects of character we have besides our drinking. Very few of us have been aware of all the defects or on some occasions were aware of at least some of these defects, but did not do anything about them. Some of these defects have become part of what I call our defense mechanism by which we excuse our actions. As an example, just think how quickly we could manufacture excuses and lies—one lie to cover up for another.

Now, after we have admitted our wrongs—be it wrong thinking or wrongdoings—in the Fifth Step, we are going to do something more than just admit or confess.

In my opinion, the words of importance are "entirely ready." Even if we have worked on Step Four and have tried to identify our defects, now is the time when we start asking for help for removal of these defects. Some people like to hang onto a few of the defects, but it is suggested that we do a complete housecleaning. I have to admit that some of the defects that give us temporary pleasure at times also have to go. We cannot, for one second, forget that we are seeking permanent sobriety for ourselves. No one can make us stop drinking. We cannot change anyone else but ourselves, so we have to come to a point of wanting sobriety. We have to become ready and willing to have God remove these defects of character.

Keep in mind that it is our character that we are working on, not the other fellow's. Here is a good place to stop the critical attitude toward others—the superior attitude that we have shown to some. We must clean our minds of wrong thinking: petty jealousy, envy, self-pity, remorse, and so forth.

We also need to drop resentments, which is one of the biggest hurdles the alcoholic has to get over. What concerns us here is that we drop all thoughts of resentment, anger, hatred, and revenge. We turn our will over to God and let His will direct us how to remove patiently, one by one, all these defects of character.

Some people—especially arrogant, self-centered people—look at their sobriety as self-inflicted martyrdom. They are, as a general rule, unable to recognize their own arrogance. Of course, they can see it in other people. They expect to be treated with respect because they are so nice and so good; but, as soon as something does not go their way, they behave like children and are impossible to live with. No happiness in sobriety can be found this way, and sobriety will not be a lasting thing. Since they are not happy, they cannot spread any happiness to other people.

Without the help of a Higher Power, our chance for success in working this step is minimal. We have to seek God, as we understand Him; and with His help find the areas where we have failed or where we have gone wrong. We will ask for His guidance for improvement in our pursuit for a better way of life.

The Sixth Step says, ". . . remove all these defects of character," and that means and includes even defects we are not aware of at this time. We have to search out the things which are slowing up our quest for sobriety. Then, we ask God's help in getting rid of these defects.

Remember, we have already dealt with these defects in our Fourth-Step inventory. Remember that we have all had resentments. We all have experienced false pride. I personally took a long time to get rid of that false pride, and it creeps up on me from time to time. We all have experienced envy and jealousy. We all have been selfish. And I think we also need to look at laziness, procrastination.

Defects of character are not things we can easily rid ourselves of, even if we recognize them. Glowing faults like false pride, selfishness, lying, lust, egotism, hate and anger—these things can only be conquered by constant effort on our part;

but first we seek out as many as possible and go to work on them, one by one. We might need to have help from outside, meaning seeking help from other people, from AA people, friends, sponsors, in order to help us overcome these defects. In many cases this may involve a trip to a pastor or our sponsor or maybe the counselor we had in treatment. We cannot just say "I have decided to get rid of my defects." It is not that simple.

I believe that we need to take a close look at what defect we identify as being the biggest and go to work on that one first of all. And, in so doing, we also somehow get to work on another defect, whether we had thought of it or not. The main thing is that we take one at a time instead of trying to overcome everything all at once. I find that to be almost impossible. I don't know if anyone has done that. I only know that I have certainly not overcome all my defects of character, but they are showing up less and less frequently than they used to. As we grow in the AA program, we find more and more of these unwanted burdens which are choking our sobriety, but, by weeding them out, we can reach new goals in our recovery.

If you have any problems in understanding this step, ask someone. Ask your sponsor. Ask an AA friend. Go and see your counselor. But ask someone to help you understand it and how to go about working out this step. There are so many adjustments that we have to make if we plan on staying sober. If we hope to get serenity and peace of mind, we need to be willing to go to any lengths and to do what is necessary for us in order to remain sober.

There is one warning that I use from time to time, and that is please do not use others for comparison. It is only ourselves we are concerned with. My recovery depends on how I work and live the program, not how other people live the program.

We need to have faith. I believe that faith is the assurance of things hoped for, the conviction of things not seen. So, I ask, do you sincerely believe that God, as you understand Him, can remove all these defects of character? Do you think he will release you from your bondage? Now is the time to ask yourself. If you do not believe that your defects can be removed, then you have given up even before you start, and you are filled with negative thoughts.

If you were hurting when you had your Fourth and Fifth Steps, then you have done some searching that went way into your past. These same defects of character that we have discussed before, you now need help with to have removed. That help we can get by sincerely, and as humbly as we can, asking God to help us remove them.

Of course, if you had four teeth that were bad and hurting, you would not ask the dentist to take only two of them out, would you? The same with our defects. If we hang on to some of them, they are going to hurt us somehow. Complete honesty with ourselves will secure our sobriety.

So, when the Sixth Step says, "Were entirely ready to have God remove all these defects of character," it means exactly what it says. Only you know when you are entirely ready. There is no sign on the outside of us that tells other people that we are entirely ready. No, only you and I know that, and, if we feel entirely ready, then we go to work and ask to have them removed. They don't go away for good—that I am convinced of—but they become less frequent in appearance. As we work on this step, we are going to improve ourselves in many areas, and our chances for continued happy sobriety are going to be more secure. So keep in mind that it is our own character defects—not someone else's—that we are working on. And, as usual, don't be afraid to get on your knees to get on your feet.

STEP SEVEN

The meaning of this step is clear. We need prayer and we need humility. No man can tell another how to pray. In my opinion, each one has, or will work out for himself, his own method. My personal opinion is that I can pray if I am lying in bed with my hands folded underneath my head. I can pray sitting "on the can." I can pray when I am driving. In general, it all depends on how humbly I am doing it. If it is just a bunch of words that are flowing out of my mouth, it isn't going to make any difference. They are not heard. I am talking about the feeling that I have inside when I pray. If that feeling is O.K., then, that's all that is needed.

If you feel that you cannot pray, my only suggestion is: Ask God to teach you how. We need to meditate. We need to have clear thoughts and clean thoughts and ask God to direct our thinking. As we have all heard many times, Christ said, "Ask and ye shall receive." So, there is no other simpler method to use. Just ask. As I said, God will teach you how. All you have to do is ask Him to teach you.

Now, I daresay that in my early sobriety, my prayers were kind of taken out of a book. They were words that were not really mine. It was more like a religious thing. But, as I grew in my spiritual life, I realized that I could use my own words, no matter how I said it—I might mispronounce a lot of them—God would understand me. And even with an accent like mine, He understands. As long as I can be as humble as I am capable of being and as sincere as I am capable of being, He will listen and He will answer.

The shortcomings we are dealing with here, in my opinion, are the same character defects that we talked about and have written down in our Fourth Step and also in our Sixth Step. But, as I see it, the Seventh Step is where we put this into action—when we have really identified these defects and shortcomings, and now we want them removed. I think of the Sixth and Seventh Steps as being something I work somehow together.

When we talk about humility, this is the virtue of being ourselves and realizing how small we really are in this big world full of its own trouble. We need to drop all pretense. We have to stop being Mr. Big Shot—bragging, boasting. We need to shed that false pride and tell the simple, plain, unvarnished truth that we act, walk, and talk simply, that we can see the little bit of good that exists even in an evil person and forget the little bit of evil that exists in a good person. I don't believe that I can afford to look down on even the very lowest of God's creatures or on man's mistakes. I also need to think clearly, honestly, fairly, and generously. I believe that the shortcomings that I am asking God to remove are the very defects of character that I used for drinking—the same defects that I drank to hide or that I drank to get away from. Every human being has character defects and shortcomings. But, since we are dealing with alcoholism, in our phase of drinking, these defects of character were showing often, and these were the defects that we so often had remorseful feelings about because we didn't like to be reminded by someone else what we had done and said the night before.

I know that some people like to meditate all alone. They like to pray alone. Personally, I can pray even in a crowded room. I don't have to move my lips. It is just that I say the words to myself inside and God will understand. As I said earlier, the defects of character, the shortcomings, don't disappear for good. So, from time to time, one of these defects will come out in the open, and then I need to pray to have them removed. None of the steps in the AA program is completed in just one sitting. None of the steps are we ever finished working at. So the same holds true with the Seventh Step. I need to continue the practice of this step. So, when these defects or shortcomings come out in the open, I need to ask, I need to pray, and I need to meditate. As the saying goes, "Humbly asked Him to remove our shortcomings." "Humbly ask *Him,*" God, as we understand God, because we are not capable of doing away with these defects by ourselves, but, with His help, they can be taken away, and then it usually ends up with their staying gone, or at least they stay away until we take over the steering wheel again and allow them back.

I do get hurt. I do get angry. I do have resentments. I do have self-pity, at times. But, as soon as I can ask for their removal, I can feel good again. We cannot afford to let these ill feelings and thoughts stay with us. We are going to be in misery if we allow that, and, the longer we allow something to stay with us (some of the character defects), the less chance we have at happiness. And, too often I'm afraid, some people will let this go on, and they end up drinking again.

Working out the suggestion of the Seventh Step is on a daily basis, like anything else that we talk about in the program. Just for today, I need to ask Him to help me overcome these defects and shortcomings. Only today do I need to have His help to overcome these defects. Being humble doesn't mean that we let someone walk all over us. Being humble doesn't mean that we become doormats. I cannot stand up and say that I feel so humble, because, as soon as I say it, then, I am not. Humility is something that we show. Something that can be seen by others, and, even if I allow the thought to come to me that I am humble, I cannot say it, because then it has lost its feeling—the feeling is gone. Often it is said by someone who receives a pin in AA: "As I stand before you feeling so humble . . ."; but I have often heard it said, and I don't really believe that the person who says it means what it really says. Humility is a feeling. Humility is something that I need but I cannot talk about. Oh yes, I have often kidded about it with friends, that I am so great and so humble, and there is a saying that, "It's tough to be humble when you are as great as I am." Well, all this can be done, as I said, in a kidding way; but, seriously, no. We cannot say, "I am humble." But I need to be humble in my affairs with God. He knows what goes on with me long before I do, and, since this step suggests that I humbly ask, then I have to arrive at that feeling of being humble. Then I can work this step. And, as I said earlier, it is only for today—one day at a time. So, before you retire tonight, remember my last words of this chapter. "Don't be afraid to get on your knees to get on your feet."

STEP EIGHT

In this step, we will make a list of all the people whom we have harmed. This step spells it out for us: "made a list." Preferably, this should be done on paper, since we are not mentally that well. Yet it will help us to put it down on paper—the names of those we have harmed.

On the top of this list, in my opinion, I need to put God. I have harmed God many, many times over—taken His name in vain, used obscenities, and sometimes used both His name and obscenities in the same sentence. I have hurt Him by abusing my own body because I am His creation. I have hurt God by abusing other people as well as His creations. Very few begin this step by thinking of the harm they have caused God. I believe that every one of us has to take a look honestly at where we have been in our relationship to our Higher Power. Haven't we all, to some degree, hurt God during our drinking?

Secondly, I believe that I need to put my own name on that list. This is also something from my experience anyway, that very few people will do. They don't think that they have harmed themselves. Oh, yes, we have. We have harmed ourselves day in and day out by the abuse of our bodies and mind. The sooner we can start to place names on this paper, the better off we are going to be, and, as time goes by, more and more names are going to come to our mind, because, as we get more mental stability and clarity, we are going to remember more and more.

Of course, some will procrastinate, saying that they will wait until some time has passed because, when the brain is clearer, then it will be easier to make out this list. To that I will say, "Bullshit." We need to get going on this, and the sooner the better. I personally began this list while in treatment, and I have added on names as time has gone by, and there are still some names on that list that are not crossed out. There are still some people that I haven't met in person. Now, we have harmed people with our drinking—intentionally and also unintentionally. In our black-outs, we have hurt someone. We can rest assured of that, even though we don't remember it. Having harmed someone doesn't necessarily mean physical abuse. We have harmed others by slanderous remarks, by having "bad thoughts" about them. It's amazing how easy it can be to hurt someone with our words, which, in my opinion, stays wide open in our drinking days. We like to put other people down and thereby build ourselves up.

I believe every step has key words, and, in the Eighth Step, I'd like to underline *became willing* and also *them all* because it doesn't say at which time in my recovery that I need to complete this step; it just says "became willing to make amends to them all." And, when it says, "to them all," it means everyone I can think of that I might have harmed. Of course, those that we are closest to and love the most we have also hurt the most. We have been used to bad mouthing our wives or our husbands, if we are married. If we are single, we might have bad-mouthed our parents, our sisters and brothers, our boss, our neighbor, our grocery-store man, our gas-station man—you name it. We had a tendency to bad-mouth most people we came in contact with, simply because they couldn't tolerate our drinking and our behavior.

In order to become willing, we need to ask God to let His will be done, not ours—and ask for the strength and the courage to become willing to forget the resentments and false pride and to make amends to those whom we have harmed. If we do this step grudgingly or as an unpleasant task to be rid of, we are in trouble already. We must do this willingly, fairly, and humbly, without any condescension.

Now, this list can become mighty long. I go back thinking about how I could harm people or kids that I went to school with. How easy it was, for instance, to break someone's pencil or to put a tack on someone's chair—be it one of the other pupils' or the teacher's. These are minor things, but I harmed people by doing it. I harmed my teachers, my fellow students, and myself. And I think of the lies that started even before drinking was a problem for me—lying was a problem, because the living situation, or rather my behavior in my living situation, had already become a problem—before alcohol became a problem. And, as I went back in my thoughts about whom I had harmed, this list grew and grew. And, as I said, there are still names that are not crossed out. We have also harmed institutions. For instance, in my case, I harmed the mortgage company that had the mortgage on our house. I harmed the gas company, electric company, telephone company, by not paying my bills. I harmed collection agencies by not going along with the agreements that I had made. So, you can see, when we honestly look at whom we have harmed, the list can be mighty long.

This is a step that I find in my experience to be of very great importance to an alcoholic if he plans on having a happy sobriety.

God's guidance is necessary. That we have to ask for. Our willingness to do what this step suggests is up to us. God will not do this for us. No one else can do it for us. I need to do this for me to secure my own sobriety. It is so easy to start thinking when we make out this list, when we think of someone we have harmed, "But that so-and-so did this to me," so I don't have to put his name down. Now, keep in mind, we are making a list of people we have harmed, no matter if they have harmed us or not. We are concerned about harm that we have done. If these other or some of these other people have harmed us, it will be up to them to make amends to us. Maybe the day is never going to come, but we are concerned about taking care of our business, our "amends-making." I believe that there are people who have harmed us, too, certainly. But that is secondary for now. We make amends to people whom we have harmed; that's number one. It might also be that some people we had harmed in the past have since died. We also need to put their names down on this list. And in the next step, we will talk about how we make amends to those people. So, don't be afraid to get on your knees to get on your feet.

STEP NINE

It is in this step I believe that we make peace with ourselves by making peace with those whom we have hurt. It says that we must make "direct amends." We must pay in kind for the hurt that we have done them. If we have cheated, we must make restitution. And, no matter how we have hurt others, we need to ask forgiveness. The list of harms done may be long, but the list of amends is equally long. For every "wrong" we have done, there is a "right" we may do to compensate.

There is only one exception. We must develop a sense of justice, a spirit of fairness, and an attitude of common sense. If our effort to make amends would create further harm or cause a scandal, we will have to skip the direct amends and take care of this matter in the Fifth Step.

Making direct amends to such people, wherever possible, means to me that I seek them out in person. Not by letter, not over the phone, but in person. I remember how filled with fear I was when I started to make amends to people. I was afraid of the rejection. I was afraid of being laughed at. I was afraid of being told to go to hell.

In order to make direct amends, there has to be a sense of humility present. Now, by this time, I am presuming that we are a little bit more honest than we were when we were introduced to the program; so we know for ourselves that we are honestly doing this for our own good and for our own recovery. And, even if it hurts and we are fearful, it needs to be done. When we are seeking out this person, or these people, and sit down and tell them why we are now coming to see them, we need to be as honest as we can, in order for them to understand why it is so important for us to go along, or go ahead, with this. We might experience being turned down, being laughed at, or being told just to disappear.

There is something I have often said, about going back to our drinking place and trying to make amends to the bartender, because we had hit him over the head with a bottle. As soon as you step into the bar, he might come around the corner of the bar, ready and willing to throw you out of the place head first. So, here we need to take into consideration what the Eighth Step said, that we "became willing to make amends." Now we will become willing to make amends, but other people might not be willing to accept our amends. There might be other situations where we will "fail" in our amends-making. I can think of my own situation, when I went back to Norway to visit after I sobered up. My sister and my brother would not, first of all, accept me as an alcoholic. Oh, sure, they knew about my drinking. They knew what embarrassment I had caused, but, every time I brought up my own problem, they were quick to find someone else who had something that was worse than what I had done, thereby trying to smooth over my alcoholism. But I could still make amends. I asked their forgiveness for the harm I had done before I left Norway. But, as I say, they did not accept me as an alcoholic. In their minds I was not "that bad."

Making amends is necessary in order for us to go on living with a clean conscience, so we don't have to walk around looking over our shoulder. We don't have to be afraid to walk places in fear of finding or meeting someone. When we make amends, we start with a clean slate. We have a fresh start on life again. There are situations that are exceptions, where maybe we need to overlook making direct amends. I have often used the example that if, for instance, a guy has had an affair with the next-door neighbor's wife; by no means would I advise him to go over and talk to her husband. That is going to create a hell of a mess in both marriages. So, something like that we take care of in our Fifth Step and are done with. We can make amends to our neighbors in this situation by remaining sober and never again attempting to have anything going with a neighbor's wife.

I have another example that I often use. A young woman who

was assigned to me in treatment was divorced. Her husband, who also was alcoholic, had left her and their two kids. This young lady worked in a grocery store, and she told me that she had stolen money (about seventy-five dollars' worth) from the till. Not all at once, but a little now and then, and she estimated it to be about seventy-five dollars. She was asking me if she should go to the manager of the store and confess this. Chances are high that the manager would not understand and she would be "black-marked." If she were to be known for stealing, she would have trouble being employed again in the field of the grocery business. My suggestion to her was to take care of it in her Fifth Step. And, if she wanted to, she could ask the clergyman's opinion, too. She later told me that the clergyman had advised her the same way I had. I am using this example because I know that most of us will have a problem in making amends where there is a situation that can be fairly sticky, where we have to use justice, fairness, and common sense.

Making amends to someone who has died was a puzzling question for me in treatment. I could not understand how I could make amends to my parents, who had both died before I sobered up. But one night my counselor sat and talked with me, and he explained to me that there was no way that I could do it in person—eye-to-eye. But he suggested that if my parents were still alive, wouldn't they be proud of me for trying to stop drinking, and to that, I had to answer "yes." He said, "Then go ahead. Make efforts at remaining sober, and believe that your parents are proud of you." Now, as my spiritual growth goes on, I have come to believe that my parents are in heaven and can see the change that has taken place with me. They can see that I am far better in my behavior and living than I ever was before. And, if they were alive, they would be proud of me. They would be proud that I have changed.

So, as of today, I remain sober and I am making amends to myself, to God, to my parents, and to everyone else, simply by being sober. I have made my restitution. I have made "direct amends" to a lot of people. But there are still people on my list, people I haven't met yet, simply because they are out of reach;

they are not in this country, and I just have to hope that I will meet them one day so I can make eye-to-eye restitution. I was in correspondence, of course, with my sister and brother long before I finally made that trip back home, but never did I attempt to make amends in those letters. That had to wait until I could do it in person. And, as I said, the day finally came.

I had a very pleasant experience making amends to both persons and institutions that I had harmed. I was never turned down and I wasn't laughed at, and I wasn't told to go to hell. The loan sharks that I had borrowed from and the companies that I owed were all willing to go along with small payments. They would assess finance charges, interest, and all that, but, they were willing to go along with small payments. There was one time when I commented to my wife that I would be on Social Security before we had finished paying these bills that had accrued the last year of my drinking. But, luckily, it didn't take that long. It took three years and two months before I had repaid the financial responsibility and the financial hurt I had caused, but it could be done. I have proven that.

We need God's help and guidance so we can determine whether it is wise to make amends at a particular time or not. We ask for His help to go on. So, don't be afraid to get on your knees to get on your feet.

STEP TEN

In coming into AA we usually will have a pretty big inventory to work on as we have done in the Fourth Step, the Eighth Step, and also in the Ninth Step. But, even so, after all that, we have not become perfect. We have a long way to go. We are going to continue to make mistakes, and we are going to be inclined to do some wrong thinking and wrongdoings for the rest of our lives. Oh, yes, we are going to continue to make mistakes simply because we are human. So, the founding fathers, who were very much aware of this, knew that we needed to take a continued inventory of ourselves, and that is why the Tenth Step is outlined as it is.

So, at intervals we continue to take a personal inventory. The purpose of this step, this inventory, is to check on our own progress. Since we cannot be perfect, we need to make a regular inventory. I hope that we keep in mind that this inventory is personal. We keep continuing to take *our own* inventory, not someone else's. We are the ones who need it—never mind the other fellow. Most likely the other fellow will also need an inventory, but we are going to let him do his own. We are concerned about ours.

It is suggested that we make this inventory before we retire at night. But, I know that some of us take four-hour spot checks just to be sure that something isn't overlooked. I have another idea, and that is that maybe a good way to start the inventory is to go over every step of the AA program and try to discover just what it is in these steps that we have not been following.

We all know that a businessman has to make an inventory of his stock from time to time. We have to make a personal inventory of ourselves from time to time if we want to recover from a serious mental disease.

We need to look at the character defects that we have written out in the Fourth-Step inventory, that we have looked upon in the Eighth and Ninth Step. We have to look at selfishness, the common vice for every alcoholic. We need to look at egotism. We have all been Mr. Big at one time or another. None of us has been without egotism. Also we have the character defect of false pride. We have been too big to admit a fault or a wrong-doing, and, certainly, we have all experienced the impatience that we have. We often refer to it as "the spoiled child in the grown man." Resentments? An alcoholic is usually sore at the whole world. Everybody else is wrong but him. Everyone else is against him. Everyone else is talking about him and trying to get him in trouble. We have been dishonest. We have tried to fool ourselves and other people—false pretense. And we have to deal with hate, jealousy, envy, laziness—the list could go on and on.

So, we have to also look at what we are to improve on. We have to show a list of virtues that we very definitely lack and should go to work on and develop, such as honesty, simple justice, fairness, generosity, truthfulness, humility, patience—again the list could go on and on.

Now, we do need to have faith. If we have lost faith, we must work hard, desperately hard, to get it back. We ask God to help us. We ask God to help us get faith back in Him. Help us get faith back in our fellowman and also in ourselves. We need to have hope. If we have lost hope, we are like dead pigeons. It is said that only those who have been cruelly hurt and in desperate need can know the wonderful sense of security that lies in hope for better things. I think you and I fit in here. We have been hurt. We have been desperate. And now that I have found the security that lies in hope, I do believe I know what I am talking about.

We also need trust. We have had a tough time trusting ourselves. We didn't trust ourselves while we were drinking, and we have a tough time trusting other people as we enter into this program. For some, it takes a long time before they are willing to trust someone else. But, you know, when I have trouble trusting someone else, it also reflects where I am at with myself: I have a low trust level with myself.

Since our own self-sufficient conducting of our own life has failed us, we must put our trust in God, Who has never failed.

I personally take this Tenth Step inventory at night. I go over in my thoughts what has taken place from the time I got up until the time I am back in bed again. I think about episodes that have taken place during the day where a comment I have made or things I have done might have hurt someone. It seems as if I keep forgetting that not everyone has the same kind of humor as I, that not everyone believes as I do. I do an awful lot of kidding, and sometimes someone takes my kidding seriously, and there is a problem which develops when this happens. I always find that I have done something wrong that I can correct the next day by watching my tongue and watching my actions.

But we also need to look at what we have done that is good. I keep fresh in my mind what so often is said, "Try to do something nice for someone without letting him know it." But, you know, every one of us has such a tough time keeping his mouth shut when he has done a good deed. We like to brag about it. We like to boast. See, the character defects are coming back, one by one, from time to time. Can you think of the last time you did something nice for someone and kept quiet about it? It's quite a tough question, isn't it?

We don't do everything wrong, and we don't do everything right in a twenty-four hour day. But I strongly believe we do more right than wrong. So, in this Tenth-Step inventory, although we look at our wrongs, we also look at what we have done right and try the best we can to make the right side become longer and longer as time goes by.

I say again, as I have said earlier, that we don't become perfect. We can strive for perfection, and we will improve ourselves through this striving, but, we will never reach perfection. I don't see anything wrong about striving for it if we keep in mind that we are never going to reach perfection. Improvements take place little by little. The harder I work, the more sincere I am, the more improvements will take place.

This Tenth-Step inventory is a spot check so we can see where we are at. I have heard it said that either we go forward or we slide back, that there is no standstill. And the Tenth Step is *the* step that we use for this guidance and checking.

I know I am far better off today than I used to be, but I am not where I would like to be. But I have a sincere belief that, as long as I keep on working at it, as hard as I keep on working at it, one day I might be where I would like to be. But, for today, I have to be satisfied with where I am at. I have to accept myself for where I am at. I have to say, "I am sorry," when I make mistakes and try to be careful not to make any more. We learn from our experiences, I hope; so, if we make a mistake today, we won't make the same one tomorrow. We need to check ourselves on a daily basis.

This is my opinion of the Tenth Step. In ending, I will, as usual, say, "Don't be afraid to get on your knees to get on your feet."

STEP ELEVEN

I believe that it is clearly spelled out for us in this step what we ought to do—"prayer and meditation."

Prayers, we have been practicing, I hope, before we get as far as the Eleventh Step. I hope we have been praying for guidance and strength, and here it says we need to continue to pray and meditate in order to gain the fullest from the relationship between God as we understand Him and ourselves.

As I have stated earlier in talking about these steps, prayers, in my opinion, can be said anywhere at any time. Now, it is also advised that we practice meditation. I personally refer to this meditation as a quiet time which I believe every one of us needs. My quiet time is usually in the morning. I get up before the rest of the family, and, during the winter months, I don't even need to turn on the lights in the kitchen, because there is a streetlight on the corner, and I get enough light into my kitchen so I can see how to make coffee. When the coffee is being brewed, I sit there at the kitchen table and I have my quiet time—my meditation. Sometimes it might be ten minutes, and other times it might be a half an hour. It is a time when I can let my thoughts flow. I can think about what I have to do today. I can think about what steps I feel I need to work a little harder on today. These are all examples that I am giving. Any one of us can choose how and where the meditation time is going to be and how it is going to be used.

I believe that it is clearly spelled out that it is through prayer and meditation that we are going to seek to better our communication with God. When it says, "Sought through prayer and meditation," that means exactly that. We need to pray. We need to meditate.

I also have found that there are days when I need to have a quiet time at work. But, I suppose that all depends upon where one is employed. The time for meditation might be a little shorter for some of us if we are going to do it while we are at work.

In order for us to improve on anything, there has to be something to begin with. For instance, when the highway department improves on the freeways, there is a freeway to begin with. They are just improving on it, and the same holds true for us. We have, by now, achieved some understanding of what our Higher Power is. In this step we are now advised on how we can improve and how we can better our relationship with that Power.

When it says, "to improve our conscious contact with God as we understood Him," it doesn't mean that we are going to walk around every day and just think about God, God, God, God. No, not at all. But it is to better our thinking by gearing our thinking along the lines of God's will for us. We are improving our living situation and our work situation by having a constant reliance upon God as we understand Him. We need so desperately to have a relationship going with our Higher Power on a daily basis. Chances are high that, without such a relationship, our days of sobriety might be numbered.

In my opinion, one does not have to be down on his knees in order to pray. In the beginning of my recovery program, I thought that is what it meant. But I quickly learned that I could communicate with my God even sitting on a chair, lying in bed, driving the car, anywhere, at any time. I have stated before that I am not religious. I preach a lot you might say, but I hope that you will bear in mind that my preaching is my own experience in this program. I know what it has taken for me and what I have needed to do to remain sober. I also know that the founding fathers of this program knew what it would take for them, and that is why they wrote the steps as they are written. The steps are the same for every one of us. It is up to you and me to live these steps as we choose. They are only suggested guidelines for recovery.

The Eleventh Step goes on to say, "praying only for knowledge of His will for us." I believe we have to have our own understanding of God's will for us. My understanding of it is that He wants me, first of all, to be sober because sober I can do something worthwhile; drunk, I am not worth anything to myself or to other people and not to God either. So God's will for me is that I stay sober. Sober I can be a little bit better husband, a little bit better father, a little bit better as a friend, as an employee, and as a citizen of this community. As a drunk I couldn't be any of these things.

So, "through prayer and meditation" I can develop a "conscious contact with God" as I understand Him, and I can pray for "knowledge of His will" for me so I can better understand what is happening. Of course, God does not come down and tell me what His will is. This is something I have to develop on a mental basis, as I understand God's will for me to be.

The step goes on to say, "the power to carry that out." I take this to mean that I pray for knowledge of His will for me and strength and power to carry out what my task in life is as I understand it to be now.

I have found this new way of living, and it has worked for me for many years. I know that by practicing this program anyone is going to benefit and make a better life for himself. So I see this as part of my task in life. Being sober I can carry this message to other people so they can have a chance to take a look at this and make a decision. If they want it, it is free.

Carrying out God's will has to be done on a daily basis. I have often referred to what I am going to say now, but to some people we are the only page of the Big Book that they will ever read. It is important how I live, because some people are going to judge AA as a whole by how I am living. This I know to be a fact. Our neighbors told us after I had been sober about six months that when I came out of treatment they were peeking through the windows behind curtains to see if I was remaining sober, and, to their surprise, I did remain sober, and their opinion of AA was strengthened by my sobriety. If I had gotten drunk, their opinion of AA would have been quite negative, I am sure. It is important how we live. It is important to us as recovering alcoholics, because we are the number-one person we are doing this for. Other people, such as our close family, are going to benefit from our sobriety, but that has to be secondary to our own recovery. I have often referred to myself and also other recovering alcoholics as being like disciples. I remember being taught when I was a child that Jesus gathered his disciples at random. He didn't go and take only the big shots and tell them to follow him. No, he chose his disciples from many walks of life. We alcoholics come from every walk of life. My personal opinion is that I think we are more from the middle class and the upper class than the "lower" class. Alcoholism does not choose just one part of the population. Alcoholism does not happen just to certain people. It is not based upon financial status. It is not based upon what religion we are. It does not depend upon what national background we have. An illness can come to anyone. We are the ones who are, to a degree, in my opinion, "picked" to become alcoholics. There has to be something with us that God finds worthwhile to proceed with. There must be a reason why I was chosen. Maybe because those of us who have suffered hell are so much more grateful for what we have found in this new way of life, and we are more up to spreading the word—going out and preaching, so to speak—to help other people. The suffering that we have been through, I see as an experience that is necessary in order to be grateful for what we have found.

The Eleventh Step is the step that has the most words of any step of the Twelve-Step program. It also has a lot of "meat" in its lines. "Sought through prayer and meditation to improve our conscious contact with God as we understood Him, praying only for knowledge of His will for us and the power to carry that out." We have a job ahead of us for the rest of our lives, a day at a time. In order to do this job the best we can, we need to also try to apply each of these steps to our lives as best we can. Practice of prayers is also going to mean that it is going to be easier and easier as time goes by to find that spot, that quiet time that is needed. It also means that we are going to have a better understanding of ourselves and God's will for us.

We are never too old to learn, and by practice we are going to improve in anything. My prayers today are not as clumsy as they were when I first sobered up. My understanding of God is far better today and more acceptable for me today than it was in the beginning. Carrying out God's will for me is a lot easier than it used to be. I have often said that I have no trouble staying sober today, but I do have living problems to deal with every day, and living problems we are all going to experience until the day we die. Life can be a lot easier to live and these living problems a lot easier to handle when we have a solid background in this program. Nobody has promised us "green acres" or that it is going to be a "dance on red roses" because we quit drinking. As stated many times before, life is not a "dance on red roses." Anything good that happens we have to work for. The same with sobriety. It has to be worked for, and the Twelve-Step program is the main thing we need to practice to achieve some peace of mind and happiness in life.

So, it is up to you and me to get to it and get going. It all depends on how much and how sincerely I want to stay sober. So, I will close with something that pertains very much to this particular step, "Don't be afraid to get on your knees to get on your feet."

STEP TWELVE

My opinion is that it is an awakening either to come into a treatment facility or to come into an AA group. We might not call it spiritual, but there is an awakening or an experience.

So many of us have thought that we were the only ones who had this problem, the only ones who were going through what we were going through. But in this group of people that we get together with, we learn that there are many others with the same problem. Some might have experienced worse things than you and I, and some others might not have experienced as many "bad things" as you and I. But yet, we have that same problem in common—our alcoholism.

I believe that there is bound to be a change that takes place for anyone trying to do what the eleven steps suggest. So, by the time we get to look at the Twelfth Step, an awakening, or a change if you wish, has taken place. Often other people are much more aware of this change than we are ourselves. Very few people with a drinking problem have taken a close look at themselves, and, by being introduced to the AA philosophy, we are bound to take a look at ourselves—what has happened in the past—to determine if we want to continue to live that way or to make a change.

In the Fourth Step, we take a look at our character defects, and we find out, at least to a degree, what we have been like, and I am willing to say that most of us would choose to change. When the Twelfth Step states, "Having had a spiritual awakening as the result of these steps," to me means that changes, even on a small scale, have taken place in the time that has been spent on working the other eleven steps. We have, hopefully, remained sober through this time. Maybe it is for thirty days. Maybe it is for sixty days. No matter what, we have remained dry, and we have had a chance to let our brains do some work.

So many of us refused the word "God." We wouldn't like to have anything to do with Steps Two and Three because they talked about a Higher Power, a power greater than ourselves, God. But, as we hung in there and listened to what other people were saying and, hopefully, did some reading of the Big Book, a change started to take place. Little by little we begin to like ourselves, and we start liking the change that is happening to us.

This step goes on to say, "we tried to carry this message to alcoholics." It does not say anywhere that because I have sobered up I am to run back to the bar where I used to hang out and try to sober up my buddies. It does not say that I have to stand on street corners and preach about alcoholism and about this new way of life that I have found. It simply says that "we tried to carry this message to alcoholics." Carrying this message can be done in many ways. I carry the message by remaining sober, by attending meetings regularly, by helping out in the kitchen of our AA club, by bringing coffee into the meeting room, by bringing ashtrays, and also emptying the ashtrays afterward.

I also believe that we carry the message to nonalcoholics. People that we have worked with—neighbors, and relatives who have been used to seeing us drunk—are going to notice the change that has taken place with us, and their impression of AA is going to be a positive one, because they are looking at us and they are judging AA by what they see happening with us. So, I often say we carry the message to alcoholics, but we also carry the message to a lot of other people. I believe the old saying of being "careful how we live, because, to some people, we are the only page of the Big Book they will ever read. I know from my personal experience that other people have been judging AA by looking at me.

One thing that is often heard in AA groups is the remark of "going on, or having been on, a Twelfth-Step call." What this means is that someone with a drinking problem has called the AA group and asked for help. Usually, in such cases, if it is a man who is calling, then a couple of guys from the AA group will go to this person's home and talk with him. That is making a Twelfth-Step call. In my opinion, a Twelfth-Step call is successful if these two AA members come back and remain sober, whether that person they went to visit comes to our AA group or not. It is a failure only if these two guys begin to drink with the one they went to see. It is recommended that there should be two of us going together on a Twelfth-Step call. I like to think that "two heads are better than one." Also, if it is a woman who calls for help, everything possible should be done to get a woman, hopefully two, to go on this Twelfth-Step call. I know that this isn't always followed and not always possible, due to the area of the country where one lives. It all depends on whether there are enough members of this group—if there are enough women members and men members. But, at least, it is suggested that a woman go on this call if it is a woman that calls for help.

Another thing that is often said is that there are no "musts" in the AA program. With that, I have to disagree. Of course, in reading the Twelve Steps as they are written, a person is not told he *must* do this or he *must* do that. But, when we read the Big Book or when we read the Twelve Steps and Twelve Traditions, we will find that there are "musts" for every one of us. I have found this to be particularly true in the reading of the Big Book. There it states over and over again what I must do in order to stay sober.

It is also of great importance for every one of us that we have a sponsor—someone who we can relate to, someone we can trust, someone who has been around for a while, someone who can teach us about this recovery program. I have noticed that at times I run into someone who is very eager to sponsor other people, going around and asking if he can be this new person's sponsor. I have always been of the opinion that it is for the newcomer to pick his sponsor. I believe that is the way it was meant to be. But, again, that is only my opinion. Sponsorship is important. Yet, there are many members of AA who have not bothered to get a sponsor or, as I have seen, many AA groups don't use personal sponsorship; but, instead, use the whole group as sponsorship. Again, I believe this is not what was intended when the founding fathers started to talk about sponsorship.

Each AA group is autonomous. Each group operates as it wishes. I cannot say that this group is doing it wrong and that that group is doing it right. No, that is not what I am saying. Each group is doing it right. No, that is not what I am saying. Each group operates as it wants to, and I believe that every AA group must be doing something right, since they have members who do remain sober, no matter how many "faults" I can find with the different groups.

In regard to carrying the message, I feel that only someone who has carried out the eleven steps that precede the Twelfth Step is capable of carrying the message. When we have done the work—what the steps suggest—we are also able to inform and explain to a newcomer how we did it, and then it is up to him whether he wants to try it or not. I cannot say to someone that he has to do it as I did. We all live the program differently, I believe; and the steps are suggested.

One thing I recommend very strongly to anyone that I meet is the reading of the Big Book. Maybe because it was so highly recommended at the place where I was in treatment is the reason I am trying to convince others how important it is to read the Big Book. I have been told that all our answers are in that book. It is up to me to read, reread, and study it.

The hardest part, in my opinion, is the last part of the Twelfth Step: "and to practice these principles in all of our affairs." What principles are we talking about? In my opinion, the principles are the steps. They are suggested, and it is up to me to do the best I can with each one.

I believe the number-one thing in practicing these principles is to maintain sobriety, and that is done only on a daily basis. Certainly, anyone can remain dry for one day. I think we have all experienced that at one time or another. So, for one day we can remain dry. As time goes by, we accumulate a few days, a few weeks, a few months and finally, we reach a year sober—something we might have thought impossible at one time. Now, we find ourselves with a year's sobriety and often it does happen that we believe that we have everything under control. Things have settled down, and we feel that we know everything and have all the answers to every question. But it isn't so. My experience has been that the old-timers that I associate with don't have all the answers, and they freely admit this. It is impressive, in my opinion, to see these old-timers, with twenty-five to thirty years' sobriety attend meetings regularly, and, upon question, they will say that they don't dare stop going to meetings. They say that they have seen what has happened to other people when they stopped going to meetings. They returned to drinking, and they are afraid that the same will happen to them if they don't continue to attend meetings. These are the people that I like to associate with. These are the people who can show me, tell me, and advise me. They have been through a lot of hell before they found AA (like you and me). But they have something that I don't have, and that is the experience of remaining sober for these many years. They can teach me, and the old saying that they taught me in my early days of sobriety was to "stick with the winners." This I have done, and I have by now accumulated some twenty-four hours of sobriety. I have always claimed only one day at a time, and, even though years have gone by since I had my last drink, I still look upon today as being the only day that I need to work at—the only day that I can be alive.

In my opinion, one can get in trouble by comparing oneself to other people, saying that he or she is not living the program as well as someone else. I think it is very difficult to judge, and what right do I have to judge? Each one of us lives the program as best he can. Obviously, someone who relapses and returns to drinking has not been practicing any of the steps. But someone who remains sober day in and day out must be doing something right. Comparison, in my opinion, can be dangerous.

I also know that the way I look upon and the way I talk about each of the Twelve Steps might differ very much from what someone else might say. My opinion of the steps is only how I see it, and I believe that every one of us has his own opinion and his own feeling about the steps; and every one of us also practices these steps his own way.

The basic way for living this program is pointed out the way the steps are written. The steps are the same for every one of us, but the practice of the steps might differ from person to person. So, by this time, when we have now started to look at what the Twelfth Step suggests, we have to look at ourselves and see if any changes have taken place, if we feel better about ourselves and about the change that has taken place, and determine if we are willing to go on to build sobriety on a daily basis, if we are willing to share with other people what we have found, and if we also are willing to go to any lengths to remain sober. That is what the Big Book says. We have to be willing to go to any lengths. That "going to any lengths" might also differ from person to person.

As I have stated in talking about the other steps, there are three things that are essential for recovery. They are H-O-W: *H*onesty, *O*penmindedness, and *W*illingness to learn and to change. If we are as honest as we are capable of being and as willing and openminded as we are capable of being, then the work has begun. Now, it is up to you and to me to continue to try to carry this message as best we can. The main thing is that we carry the message by remaining sober, first of all. All the other things that need to be worked at will come about slowly. We need to practice patience. Rome was not built in a day. We are not going to recover in a day. We do not turn into saints. We do not become religious. But, by practice of these principles, changes will take place, and we will become better people for ourselves and our families and also for the community as a whole.

I wish you the best of everything in your striving for recovery, and as usual, I will close with: "Don't be afraid to get on your knees to get on your feet."

THE "SERENITY PRAYER"

I believe that most alcoholics, whether they have been showing a perfect church attendance or not, after a few months in AA, eventually come to realize they do need to rely on a *Power greater than ourselves.*

Some people seem to grasp the spiritual part of the program very quickly, but others will struggle for a long time before they finally reach what I call *the "surrender period."*

Every person in this room has problems of some kind, and most of us have come to see that there are really only two courses open: *"either to change and solve the problem by action,"* or *"to accept them as they are and remove them from our conscious mind."* To remain in the middle—undecided—will only produce more confusion, more problems and unhappiness.

I believe that the most important factor in approaching *all* problems is to know *when to change* and *when to accept.*

Somewhere along the line in AA's history, the so-called "Serenity Prayer" came along. I do not know for sure where it came from or when. I have heard from some sources that it goes back to the Old Testament, but I have had not any proof of that. Again, this is something I have to *accept,* since I do not know, and I believe that it really does not matter to us who wrote this prayer.

Please understand that what I say is my own understanding of it.

Let us take the first sentence: "GOD, GRANT ME THE SERENITY." Anyone who says this prayer must have some opinion of *WHO* he is addressing if he uses the word GOD! That is Whom I believed in as a child, and that is Whom I believe and trust in today.

GOD, AS I UNDERSTAND HIM, IS OUR FATHER, POWERFUL, FORGIVING, LOVING. Somewhere in the Bible it says: "Everything is possible to him who believes." I was brought up to believe that GOD would *forgive* ALL my sins.

A loving God: Jesus Christ told us "Whatever we ask in His name will be given to us," and by using the word *Grant,* I believe that I am asking for a gift. I feel that when I say, "GOD GRANT ME," then I also need to accept what I get, but I have trouble in this area at times, *especially when God's answer is NO!*

I also think of what we say in the Lord's Prayer: "Forgive us as we forgive others," but my opinion is that if GOD were to forgive me as I forgive others, I would not yet have any feelings of being forgiven.

Because HE *loves* me, he forgives! ME? Who am I? A sinner of the worst kind, an alcoholic, a cheater, a liar! How can I expect forgiveness from anyone? Let's be sure of *one thing; God makes no deals.* He does not say that I have to do certain things before *He* will forgive me. *He* forgives the first time I ask, that is, *if* I sincerely believe in *God.*

Often an alcoholic will feel worthless, guiltridden from past behavior, and has a tough time accepting that someone cares. He also will have problems trusting other people, simply because he does not trust himself. So I ask myself: "Am I worthy of *God's* forgiveness? Have I done anything good in life?" The answer to all of us is *yes.* We are basically good, but show "bad" behavior at times. *God* forgives us whoever we are or whatever we have done.

It is said that serenity means more than happiness, more than peace of mind, more than contentment.

Happiness is having what we want, for now.

Peace of mind is absence of conflict in mind—no worries, no problems unsolved.

Contentment is being satisfied with what we have, meaning I accept what I have, even though I might not like it!

I saw it written somewhere that serenity is "That peace which surpasses all understanding." I don't even understand that sentence! I believe that serenity means that I can remain *undisturbed,* no matter what happens around me, and let me quickly say: *That* I am *not* capable of doing. As we read in history books, we find people with serenity that we might envy. There has always been someone with this serenity, and there are people like that today, but I know that I will never have, never accomplish such serenity as Jesus Christ had, as he hung on the cross for three hours. Remember what *He* said: "Father, forgive them, for they don't know what they do."

To me, only *God* can be *perfect* in anything; only GOD can be *complete.*

But I continue, day in and day out, to say, "GOD, GRANT ME THE SERENITY, TO ACCEPT THE THINGS I CANNOT CHANGE." This word *ACCEPT* comes into my life so many times every day.

I need to accept myself for what I am,
I need to accept others as they are, and
I need to accept circumstances!

Yet, I do not succeed every time I try, and I believe the reason for that is that I am not *willing—really willing! To accept* means that I can say, "Yes, Father," anytime, about anyone or anything, *but* I have to *mean* it. Acceptance means to do, willingly, what we believe *God* wants us to do. So, I could say, "O.K., God, I'll try," without attempting to change other people, things or circumstances.

TO ACCEPT THE THINGS I CANNOT CHANGE: I believe that *things* here refers to everything; people, material things, everything that exists! *No* exceptions! *Change* means either to *eliminate* or to *make different,* so it no longer concerns us.

Do I live up to what I am asking God? NO. I do not like or accept myself all the time, I do not have clean thoughts all the time; neither do I feel at ease all the time. Not always do I accept people or circumstances as they are, and there are times when I do not accept *God's* way of doing things. Example: *my will* vs. *God's will.*

For a long time I believed that *courage* meant *to dare,* for example: that I could *dare* get up and speak in front of people. But, as I read in books of all kinds, I have found that *courage* means "Determination in spite of fear," *not* the absence of fear. I can think of how I felt when going around to different people and businesses and companies, making amends; *then,* even without knowing it at the time, I had courage. I was scared like hell to face these people, filled with fear, and yet I went ahead and met them eye to eye to make amends.

By saying, "GOD GRANT ME THE SERENITY, TO ACCEPT THE THINGS I CANNOT CHANGE, THE COURAGE TO CHANGE THE THINGS I CAN," I feel that what I am really asking is for *God* to give me the *willingness to do* and the *strength to accomplish,* whatever it is, no matter how fearful I am.

We ask *God* to grant us *wisdom.* Wisdom is not knowledge, but the ability to see the truth and find the correct course to follow. Maybe I could say that *wisdom* is *knowing what to do with knowledge. A wise person* is usually one who goes *contrary* to so-called popular, modern trends, but, at the same time, he knows what truth is and lives by it. I have read that there are only two sources of wisdom in life: one is age, the other a gift from God.

Youth, in itself, cannot have *wisdom!* We can see it in our everyday living, that most organizations select an older person to lead. *Example*: In order to run for president, you have to be at least thirty-five years old!

If we want wisdom, it may come to us with age, and I believe strongly that wisdom will also come as an answer to sincere, humble prayers.

TO KNOW THE DIFFERENCE. *To know* means to be able to draw definite conclusions, to be conscious of, and to have the facts. In order to get the facts, I have to do some work, some digging, some asking, and some reading. I cannot sit and wait for information that I need; I have to go out and look for the facts.

I know that AA works; that is a fact. Yet I do not understand why. There is no reason why AA should work! Ex-drunks getting together on a weekly basis and remaining sober! But it works; we are the proof!

I need to try to find the best course to take, the best decision to make, the correct action! But I need help with this, and I get that help by *praying,* but again I like to add: I do not always do the right things; I goof quite often.

TO KNOW THE DIFFERENCE I understand as "to act to change something, or to relax and accept things as they are."

1. Most things outside ourselves, be they people or circumstances, *we cannot change.*
2. Most of the things inside ourselves, be they attitudes, thinking, or feelings, *we can change.*

It is said that, "if you feel farther away from *God* today than yesterday, don't make any mistake about *who* moved." I always get a kick out of hearing someone say "I can't find God." My answer: I did not know *He* was lost!!!

Honesty, willingness, and openmindedness *are essential* for recovery from alcoholism, and on page 60 of the Big Book it says: "We are not saints. The point is that we are willing to grow along spiritual lines. The principles we have set down are guides to progress. We claim *spiritual progress,* rather than spiritual perfection." I believe very strongly in reading of the Big Book, and I have been told that all our answers are there. The Recovery Program is in the first 164 pages, it is up to me to read, reread and study it.

What I was told and advised at Pioneer House, I firmly believe in. Among other things, they advised me to read from the Big Book every day, even if it was only one page I read. I have tried to live as I was advised, and things have worked out fine for me most of the time.

At Pioneer House, they promised me that if I would take their advice, and try to live the program a day at a time, then I would *never* need to take that first drink. So far I have not taken that first one, but I have come close on two occasions. Both times I got out of the "stinkin' thinking" by praying, so I have experienced getting help from God when I needed it badly.

I make lots of mistakes. I sin every day, and yet, I feel that God loves me, because I get strength from Him to go on, to try to improve.

It would not amount to much if all we were after was to stop drinking. Sobriety is more than just being dry. Sobriety is only a bare beginning; it is only the first gift of the first awakening that we have. If more gifts are to be received, then our awakening has to go on. As it does go on, we find that, bit by bit, we can trade in the old life, *the one that did not work,* for a new life that *can and does* work under any conditions.

Let me close by using a saying which I learned at Pioneer House: "Don't be afraid to get on your knees, to get on your feet."

THE "MASTERY" OF SOBRIETY

In order to be good at, or to "master" anything, we need to practice. Repeat, repeat, and repeat.

It would be nice if there were such a thing that once we had learned to "Master" something, there would not be any need for practice, but it does not work that way.

We do know that any *master,* be he in music or sport, needs to continue to practice in order to stay a "master." All of us know someone famous, either by reading about him, or personally. Somehow, someone gets to be a little bit better than others in the field. It is at this *certain thing* that he is better that makes him so outstanding. Take a name like Babe Ruth. For years now, his name and his number of home runs, 714, has had some magic to it. Chances are that Hank Aaron's name will be mentioned more in years to come.

But some famous people are at the top for a while, and then they fade. *Why?* A well-known violinist, who had been through the "failure" part, talked about his thoughts before he began to fade; he said, "If I fail to practice one day, I shall notice the difference in my playing. If I fail to practice two days, my family will know, and, if I fail to practice three days, my public will notice."

It is the same with the alcoholic who fails to practice. Soon someone will notice that he is not practicing the program.

It is only by practicing that these "old-timers" achieve so many years of sobriety, even though life has handed them a lot of rotten stuff. The program is repeat—repeat—repeat, but this kind of repeat keeps me out of jails and drunk tanks; this kind of repetition has helped me become a little bit better person.

Hopefully we all know and understand that we are never to

become perfect, yet we can strive for perfection. In this striving, we will learn to master certain things, like some of our character defects, to a degree.

Only by practicing the program as best we can will any improvements come about. I believe that it does not matter if I attend seven meetings a week and read the Big Book every night; if I do not try to *live* the program, and practice the program, I will fail. Again, it tells me *repeat*—repeat.

We hear about those who have been sober for a while, maybe for years, and then suddenly they are drinking. What happened? Why do AAs slip? Why does the old-timer in AA disappear from our ranks?

All these questions can be answered with one sentence. "They stopped practicing." Some say "I have learned AA. I learned the Twelve Steps." "I learned everything about alcoholism and the alcoholic." But they forgot, or stopped practicing, all what they had "learned."

The Twelve Steps are, and have to be, important in maintaining sobriety, for retaining the "mastery" in sobriety.

They never learned, or they neglected the truth, that "to practice these principles in all our affairs," means to repeat and repeat, day in and day out.

Every "slipper," every unhappy person in AA has never accepted, or has not continued to apply, what I feel to be the most important part of the program: "to practice these principles in all our affairs." I am not referring to the Ten Commandments or the Principles of Justice, and so forth. I am referring to the application of these same old truths to the alcoholic problem, the principles that "worked" for someone else can also work for me, *if I am willing!!!*

The principles that someone handed to me when I sought help was that the only hope for freedom from the slavery of alcoholism would be *complete abstinence.*

But they also told me that it all would depend upon me, how much I wanted to stop drinking. Total sobriety depends upon honesty, willingness and openmindedness. But being sober and living the program to the best of my ability, I still have many problems to work out.

Everyone has problems of some kind. I call my problems, "the pains of being alive." Both the alcoholic and his family have suffered pains through the drinking years, but some pains don't stop just because drinking stops. There are so many pains we suffer every day, every one of us. Living problems that we all have to face can be very painful at times.

The pains of growing up we have suffered—for example, the baby who's trying so hard to walk across the living room, how many times does he fall down before he finally "masters" that walk. But the baby learns a few things by trying again and again. We all need to be willing to learn from pain and hurts.

The alcoholic who suffers like hell coming off a bender swears up and down that it is going to be different next time, but as we all know . . .

After some period of sobriety, the living pains might be overwhelming one day, and, knowing from past experience that drinking will take pains away for the moment, the alcoholic takes that first deadly drink. Pains go away, and hopefully will never come back.

But reality does not disappear for good; that we have seen and experienced, and we find out that there are many pains we had better learn to accept. This word, *acceptance,* comes into my life frequently, not only in the First Step. There are things about me that my wife does not like, and there are things about her that I don't like. Yet we need to try to accept each other for what we are. Feelings we have need to be expressed, but sometimes, *maybe too often,* we do not have the guts to "tell it like it is." We are afraid to hurt others' feelings, *we say,* but the truth is that we are afraid that the other person might *not like us or accept us!*

Basically we don't give a damn for *their* feelings, but we try, at times, to justify our feelings, actions, even our thoughts.

I believe the biggest pain I suffer is when things don't go *my way,* self-pity. I often talk about that little boy in me that comes out in the open from time to time, especially during moments of self-pity and resentment.

Basically nobody can hurt me. I allow myself to feel hurt. I am the only one who can control my feelings, yet I find myself saying at times, *he or she* made *me feel so and so.* My feelings—only I can control!!

It hurts when we have planned something, but then something else happens, and our plans go down the drain. It hurts when someone close to us dies, and it hurts when we hear of someone who has returned to drinking. There are, as I said, so many pains and hurts, every day, yet, we *survive!*

Feelings we have are not always easy to deal with. We might know right from wrong, yet not always want to follow the right way, because our feelings are so strong the other way. We are led by our feelings. At times we hurt *with* someone, and other times we hurt because of what someone else said or did.

I feel pretty sure that most of us have secretly had a feeling that we did not dare to express, and some of us still have feelings that cannot be expressed, at least I do. Take the feeling of love. How do you explain that to someone? I feel it is very hard to explain, that love has to be experienced in order to be understood. At times I have feelings of wanting something, the feeling of *desire,* and at times I have wanted or desired what belongs to someone else. I cannot have it, yet I allow myself to keep that feeling of desire and also the pain that comes with it.

When we learn to accept ourselves and our feelings a little better than before, then it is also easier to accept others' feelings. A feeling I have, only I can deal with, only I can decide what to do with. And I am the only one who knows if I can be comfortable with it. Maybe something I do is not accepted by someone else, but, as long as I can be comfortable with the way I live, that is all I need to know.

Many things in our society might not be what we like, but it would be a Hell of a mess if we were to behave insanely when there was something we disliked. It is really surprising how much pain and suffering we human beings can take before we give up.

I tell myself this quite often: "I can take this and *much more.*" Being oneself, accepting oneself, can be difficult and painful, but trying to live up to other people's expectations of us is a lot more difficult. We then will have to become phoney and put on a show.

Liking myself, accepting myself, I see as an important factor in recovery from alcoholism. But, I do *not accept* myself all the time, and I am *not comfortable* all the time. I have had times when I have questioned whether life was worth living, moments when I questioned if I really were an alcoholic, other times I have questioned if I were in the right line of work. These negative thoughts tend to sneak in when I have a gray day, and I do have my gray days. *Period.*

I have found that it is important for me to talk to someone about my feelings, and, good or bad, I need to express these feelings. But I also feel we should choose carefully *whom* we like to talk to.

I feel it's important that this person understands, not necessarily gives advice, but understands. We are so afraid, at times that we are going to be rejected. The one who suffers the most is *I,* when I do not say what I am really feeling. Many feelings I have had and continue to have today, I have to go to God with. I ask His guidance and help. I ask if this is His will for me, is this really supposed to happen to me, and I find myself waiting for the answer. Sometimes I question if He heard me, and other times I say He did not answer, but what I often refuse to accept, is that God can also answer with one word: *NO.*

I try, as best I know how, to live the way I can be comfortable, *most of the time,* but I say again: *I am not always comfortable, and I do not always like myself.* Life is a learning experience. We could, maybe, say it is a trip we take and that we are going to learn a lot on the way. Honesty, willingness, and openmindedness are the three things they told me that would be necessary in order for me to have a chance.

One thing we preach over and over again is self-honesty. I can only be as honest as I am capable of being at this point, I will *never* achieve complete honesty. I am basically honest, but dishonest thoughts, dishonest words, and dishonest behavior sometimes take over.

That does not mean I am bad! People are basically good, but do bad things at times. I am convinced that, in order for me to stay alive, my best chance is to try to live the AA program to the best of my ability. I am convinced that without AA I would be dead by now. As long as I can stay with and hang onto what I believe in, then, *most* of the time, I will also feel better about myself and also about others.

Remember Mary Magdalene in the Bible? She was a prostitute, a common ordinary prostitute, when Jesus met her, but she was an honest prostitute. There are two kinds of prostitutes. One type does it for money; she sells her body for cash, does not care who her partner is, as long as he can pay. The other kind, the minority of prostitutes, consort with men because they want to do exactly that. They are not in business because of family background; neither are they forced into prostitution, nor are they in this business for money, but simply because they love it!! To some people this seems odd, but it's honest!! And isn't it strange that Jesus chose to show himself to her, after resurrection, even before He showed Himself to Peter and the others? Jesus said of her, "She has loved much." Some might say that what she had been doing was wrong, but can anyone say that it was dishonest?

"The one who sins, and knows and admits that he sins, can, and probably will, merit peace, grace, serenity, and salvation. But the one who sins and will not admit to it, has not got a chance, for he has nothing to be saved from."

Our primary job in life is *us,* but we have a lifetime to do it. "Mastery" is not achieved in one day, or one month, or one year, but only by continued practice, repeating and repeating.

I am not capable of handling more than today, and, at times, I do not even feel capable of that. I am never going to be perfect, I know that. I preach a lot about honesty, and yet I do not always live up to what I preach and believe in. (Sometimes I still speed on the highway.)

I can give advice how to do this and that, which is easy. We all give advice to someone almost every day, but the one we give the advice to, he is the only one who can decide if he is going to follow our advice. There is a saying that I like very much. It goes like this: "Don't walk in front of me, I might not follow. Don't walk behind me, I might not lead. But walk by my side, and I'll be your friend."

Life will at times offer us some bad deals, but for today we can handle even the *heaviest burden.*

So for tomorrow and all its needs, I no longer Pray,
But guide me, Lord, and keep me JUST FOR TODAY.
Don't be afraid to get on your knees, to get on your feet.

SPIRITUALITY

When we were drinking, most of us never gave a split second's thought to being of help to someone else.

Sure, while hanging out at the bar, we were of great help to our drinking pals, buying drinks for the whole room or giving advice on whatever was being talked about. We were the greatest in everything: history, music, football, baseball, whatever. We had read everything about it, we had played on big teams, we were big shots—no question about it.

In my case, being a painter, I also had my own business for a while, but drank myself out of it. I could sit or stand up at the bar and talk about these big projects I was running, how many men worked for me, what a big payroll I had, what a terrible home life I had because I was so busy in my work. Drinking problems? No!

So we come into AA and discover that helping others is part of our life. We feel happy by being available to others. We go to any extent to be of help, because that's how our own sobriety is secured. It really makes me feel bad when I go on a "Twelve-Step call" and discover the alcoholic father lying on the floor or on the sofa, when a bunch of children are around, not really knowing what's wrong with their father. Perhaps they will think like this: "Just a couple of days ago he was so good to us, took us to the ball game, bought us everything we asked for at the park, and now, now he's a different man; he doesn't want us around. He yells at mother, threw the dog outside, burned a hole in the chair, and called us names." As the "Big Book" says, "Why do we let those we love so much suffer so long?" Wives and children do not always understand why we were so completely changed when we were drunk. We help a guy to AA, and he stays sober for a while; then "boom"—there he goes again.

Nobody's fault but his own, but still it hurts you. Wife and children lose faith in him, sometimes in AA, too, but we shall never say: "He is not ready yet." Who are we to decide if that man or woman is ready or not? How can we sit in judgment?

I feel that a lot of time was spent on me by others, especially my sponsor, and I'm just repaying this when I'm helping someone else to find this new way of life. AA is not mainly sobriety, but a way of life. But sobriety has to come first, because, if I'm not sober, what will happen to my family? Sobriety has to be number one for every alcoholic.

If you are unhappy in your sobriety, your days of sobriety are very few. Happiness has to accompany your newfound sobriety; otherwise, it doesn't work. It is a *must* to me to say a prayer every morning, asking for help and guidance for that day. I also say thanks at night. The benefits you get from living a sober life are so many. I add them all up in one word: *happiness.*

You have heard it said that you take out of life what you put into it. You also get out of AA what you put into it, plus interest. In AA, the interest is paid daily, but even if we had thirty years of sobriety, we could not live on the interest alone. We have to attend the meetings—that's our deposit. Some of us deposit a meeting every night, some once a week; others attend a meeting a month. But we don't have to worry about what others do, about what others say, or how often they come to meetings. We just make sure we are there at the meeting and that we get our interest. This is a selfish program, you know, and we have to take care of ourselves first.

Set a good example for others by continued sobriety, attending meetings, being available. Do not tell a new man that he has to live without liquor the rest of his life. That will scare him. We do not think in long terms like that, just twenty-four hours at a time. Some of us have to break it down to twelve hours, eight hours, maybe one hour; but, sooner or later, it's going to hit you that if the rest of these people can live this way, you're going to try, too.

Yesterday is gone. Tomorrow is not here yet. Today is the day that is important.

I don't mean to say that as soon as a person becomes an AA member, all his problems are solved. No, sir! It's far from that. We have many, many problems, each one of us, but one problem we have in common, and that's why we come here, why we stay, why we like it here. Here in AA, we have found what we thought never existed. Here we have found friends we trust, people who talk the same language we do.

Tell a new man to keep an open mind and to take it easy. Not every one of us who has been sober for a while understood everything we heard. I still learn. Every meeting I attend I learn something.

This is a simple program, and, if you think it isn't for you, just lower yourself down to my level and you'll see it works.

The spiritual part of the program was placed there because it was necessary. If you think differently, that's your problem. I believe in God. I have a great faith in Him, because I have seen His help come to me when I needed it. Without my spiritual help and guidance, I would not be here talking tonight. Nowhere under the sun is there a group of people *more in need of spiritual guidance than we alcoholics* who have given up the booze.

Psychologists turn to religion because they find out that knowing about ourselves is not enough. We need a faith in something stronger outside ourselves. The strength that comes from faith in God is not to be measured. Our willpower is nothing compared to His strength. People are weak, but God knows what is best for us.

The friendship in AA is something that has to be experienced in order to understand it. Somehow we are tied to the other members with things we do not see. But the Big Book warns us about putting one man up there as an idol. I do admire people for their length of sobriety. I respect their sobriety. All of us stay sober for twenty-four hours at a time. Even nonalcoholics cannot live for more than twenty-four hours at the time. I do not know what tomorrow will bring. Maybe there will not be any tomorrow for me. I feel I'm here on earth on borrowed time, and, if I were supposed to know the future, I would have been made that way. Only One knows what lies ahead and that is Our Heavenly

Father and then it is just plain common sense to let Him take care of us for twenty-four hours at the time.

It does strike you, when you see that a man becomes a living human being again after all he has been through as a drunk. The help from "up above" works through people. We who have gotten this second, maybe the last, chance at life again, set the example for the new person who seeks help. A salesman has to believe in what he sells. We have to believe in what we *give away*. Yes, it's all free, and we can take it or leave it. God is always there to give us help. All we have to do is pray. Ask God to teach you.

"AA is for those who want it, not for those who need it." Everyone I came in contact with knew that I needed help, but, as long as I did not want it, there was nothing to be done. If you think AA is for you, stick with us. If you think that we have nothing for you, come back anyway. If you came to this meeting, that means you *think* you have a problem, and you are certainly welcome. You are most welcome to visit us again because we have something you do *not have,* and, if you want it, you'd better come around, and it's free. Some people think they can handle booze after a short (or long) time of sobriety. They try, and, most certainly, end up here again or in a hospital or in a cemetery!

Once an alcoholic, always an alcoholic. You hear about someone falling off the wagon, and you feel sorry for him. You seldom hear about John or Tom who came in through this door many years ago and is still dry. They call it a "slip"; that is a nicer word for drunk. It's all thought about a long time before it happens. Think dry; stay dry.

I feel that, when a guy has been drunk after some time of sobriety, that man is as new to the AA program as I was when I came to the first meeting. Somewhere along the line, that man has failed and should find out where to prevent further occasions like this.

"Stick with the winners" was said to me by one of the founders of our AA group. I *do* stick with winners. I do stay sober. I do make myself available. I do attend meetings. I do believe in a Power greater than myself.

Every morning when I wake up, I'm a potential drunkard for that day, and that I know. That's why I ask for help and guidance from God. We do have a choice—a choice which each one of us has to make for himself every day. We know the good things that have happened to us since we joined AA. We know the bad things that happened to us when we drank. Make a choice for yourself.

If I had not gotten help when I asked for help, I would not try to preach as I do. But I know that we come here to get help, and there is only one way to get it. Surrender to the fact that we are powerless over alcohol; believe that a power greater than ourselves can straighten out our thinking; continue to take an inventory of ourselves; and try to bring this message to other alcoholics who are still suffering.

A new man who comes into an AA meeting and hears the laughter and sees all the smiling faces can hardly understand that this is AA. We, who have been dry for some time, can laugh at the many, many stupid things we did while drunk, but I tell you, the first two or three months I was dry, I did not talk about or laugh about my foolishness as a drunk. What's done is done. Gone is gone. But it is good when we can talk and laugh about it.

We are not perfect in AA, but we try to do our best. The Twelve Steps are suggested for us on our way to recovery. They have to be worked at if we want any satisfaction out of the program. Some people have tried to pick the steps apart, only to find out that it does not work. They (the steps) are here to stay.

This chapter was based upon what the *24 Hours a Day* book says on my birthday, my wife's birthday, my daughter's birthday, and my boy's birthday. This little book, *24 Hours a Day,* is of great help to me, and I want everyone to get one and read it. You get the feeling that they are writing about you at times.

Practice of Steps Two and Three I have found to be of great help to me. It's not easy, but nothing good in life comes easy. We have to work for it. God forgives us the first time we ask His forgiveness. So, "don't be afraid to get on your knees to get on your feet."

A NEW WAY OF LIVING*

My name is Svenn. I'm an alcoholic and I'm proud to be a member of Alcoholics Anonymous because through AA I have found a new way of living. I came here from Norway not knowing I had a drinking problem. Through drinking I lost my self-respect and respect from others. I almost lost my family, and I almost lost my house. I lost my business, and, when I came to AA I was broke—financially, spiritually, mentally, and physically. I am glad I got a second chance at life and had my three weeks at Pioneer House.

My dear wife was born in this country, but we met in Norway. We have a daughter and a son. We have a home, which I own the front door of, and the mortgage company owns the rest, but we have each other, and we have faith.

I would like to make it clear before I start my talk, that I do not look upon myself as a religious man. I preach a lot, some will say, but what I say and what I preach is strictly the way I feel—not how *you* have to do it. This philosophy has worked for me, and maybe something of what I say will help someone else. I found out one thing in AA and that is that here we can do *together* what I could not do *alone,* and that is staying sober.

When I came into AA, I was sick and tired of living the way I was living—sick of being sick and tired all the time. I did not dare to sober up because then I would get sick. *So, the last four months of my drinking, I was not sober one day.* I can remember telling my wife that I drank so much because I was an alcoholic. I used it as an excuse. Really, inside me, I knew something was wrong since I did not have the power to stop after a couple of

*This is a talk I gave at an AA meeting.

drinks as I had planned to. How many times I had planned to have just a couple and then leave and instead ended up closing the bar. I did not understand why this was happening to me. I was more interested in drinking than anything else. Work started to interfere with my drinking. I came to AA and could not be sure who was an alcoholic and who was not. All the people looked like nice business people to me. But, since I was not fully convinced that I was an alcoholic, I tried drinking again, and then I ended up at Pioneer House. *Thank God, we have a place like Pioneer House to go to for people like me. At Pioneer House, I found myself, and I also found God, as I understand Him.*

I admitted I was powerless over alcohol and that I could not manage my life. *I later made sure that I really surrendered to Step One, not only up in my head, but I let my guts know it, too!!*

I have a great faith in my Higher Power, and some people say I am a preacher. What I say, or preach if you wish, is only to tell you how I work the program *and not to tell you how to live.* I believe that we have to work the program the way it's best for us.

"First things first," we say, and to me first thing is my sobriety. *Without my sobriety, I am lost; I am a complete nothing!*

I believe it takes a big man to accept and surrender to Step One. Of course, I did not think so when I attended my very first meeting, but, after I surrendered, I came to believe that I had made the biggest decision in my life. My sobriety comes before my wife and children, before my boss and friends. If I should take that first drink, only God knows what would happen. *"Nothing is so bad that a drink cannot make it worse."*

We all have another drunk coming, if we want it; *but do we have another recovery coming?* I do not want to find out. As long as I can stay on the beam I am on, my thoughts will be *dry, because I think dry.*

I am powerless over alcohol, but also *my wife is powerless over alcohol.* She is not an alcoholic, but there is absolutely *nothing* she can do if I should decide to start drinking again! I have said it so many times how grateful I am for Al-Anon and the great way Al-Anon members are helping each other. *They need Al-Anon just as much as I need AA.* I need AA very much, because through AA I found a new way of living. And I do not want to lose what I have gained. My whole life depends upon my sobriety, and, the more I am exposed to AA, the more I learn, the more I gain, and life seems to smile more often.

This morning, when I woke up, I was a potential drunkard for today, *but I had a choice. We all have this choice to make, and for me it is very easy to choose.* I look back and see what happened to me while I was drinking, and then I see what has happened since I joined AA. My choice is easy!!

I look upon AA as a bank. My meetings are my deposit. The more meetings, the more I deposit. Then, of course, when I deposit, I can draw interest, and my interest is paid daily. *I can never deposit enough,* but strangely enough, *it seems as if the more interest I draw, the more there is to draw from.* They say you get out of the program what you put into it. I believe I am drawing more out than I am putting in. I try to practice AA in all my affairs but, on the other hand, *I am only human.*

We are no saints in AA. Only one Man was perfect, and they put *Him* on a cross. I have a very short fuse at times, and I think that my temper is one of my biggest shortcomings. But I am aware of it, I try to control it, and I feel I am making progress.

I have found true friends in AA. Those friends I had next to me at the bar have not yet made an effort to find out how I am. Really, I cannot remember the names or faces anymore, and I don't want to look back into that matter anyway. But, if I am not at the club *one* night, a lot of people call to find out why. There are three nights a week that I am at our club, and I miss very few meetings. *We do care about each other in AA.* I feel as if we are tied together by strings we do not see, but somehow we feel attached to one another. *We do care about each other!*

I am an alcoholic, and I will die an alcoholic. I do not care to find out what caused me to drink or why I became an alcoholic. I know that I have the disease of alcoholism, and I have found the way *to arrest it.*

I have accepted and surrendered to Step Number One. Some of the guys I am sponsoring did not have to go to a rehabilitation center as I had to. They came to the club, are still coming, and they are still sober. Others go to hospitals, rehabilitation centers, and in and out of AA, and yet they cannot find what we have found. They want AA and what we have; otherwise they would not come back, and *I have never said that "he or she is not ready yet." How can I judge?* How can I say when they are ready? Only One knows our future and what is in store for each of us.

This program cannot be pushed upon anyone. Neither can I push the spiritual part of the program upon anyone. I think I really got to depend upon a Higher Power after I had an experience when I had about three months of sobriety. I prayed for God's help to straighten my thinking, to help me *not* to take that first drink, and He did, and I have not had any temptations like that since. I knew He would help me if I asked, if I asked sincerely and humbly for His help. While drinking, I promised God anything and everything if I could get out of the jam I was in, but I never kept my promises. *I will say one thing, though:* When I promised my wife I would not drink anymore, I really meant it, but, when I saw the flashing "Hamm's" sign, I forgot all about my promises. I was powerless over alcohol, and I knew it.

If someone should ask you *if AA works,* answer this way: *"Is the Pope a Catholic?" Of course, AA works! We are many, many examples in this room to prove it.* But we have to *want* it. Everyone knew I needed AA while I drank, but since I did not want it, there was nothing anyone could do.

Rumors fly easily through the air, and because of this you will always hear about those who have a relapse or "slip," as they call it. *But remember also that you seldom hear about Tim or Tom, who came into the program many years ago, and is still dry.* These people with years and years of sobriety got it only by staying sober *twenty-four hours at a time.* How easy it is when you can say that I will not drink today. Maybe tomorrow and tomorrow you'll say the same thing again. Twenty-four hours at a time seems to work!

If you don't think this program is simple to follow, then go ahead and drink some more. *Eventually, the alcohol is going to damage your brain, so you can see how simple it is.* Come down to *my* level, and the program will seem simple for you also.

I tell every new man in AA to "keep an open mind." That's what my sponsor told me, and I repeat it over and over again. No one can understand everything the first or second or third time he comes to meetings. But give it a try. Hang around long enough to give the program a chance. You see, *we who are on the program have something you don't have,* and, if you want part of it, you have to come to meetings to get it, and most of all: *"It's free."* We can show you the tools you have to work with. *You* have to do the footwork *yourself.* These tools we can give you free, and, if they fit your hands, you'll use them to your satisfaction and then show others.

We are very fortunate, we who have found this new way of life through AA. We have a lot to be grateful for, a lot to say thanks for.

I have two kids, a daughter and a son, and neither one ever saw me drunk. I am so grateful to God for giving me these children and wanting me to become an alcoholic so I could find a new life and a better way to live with my family. The feeling I have inside me for my children cannot be explained. It's something that grows day by day. Now I know what it is to be a husband and father. My daughter asks every night at the supper table, "Who's coming tonight to babysit?" It seems to her that my wife and I are gone every night, but it is not really so. My daughter knows we go to the club to a meeting, but, of course, she has no idea what kind of a meeting. At least, she grows up knowing that I go to meetings very often, so maybe when we can explain AA to her it will be easier than we think.

Another piece of advice I'd like to give you is this: *Don't try to pick the steps apart!* I have seen it so often when people try to take the steps apart to fit them and their thinking, they end up drunk. *I believe the steps were made the way they are because the founders knew what it would take to make it work.* So, please, take my advice; leave the steps the way they are. Someone said the steps are like a smorgasbord, and I say: *Well, if it is a smorgasbord, then I'll have a taste of everything. I do not want to leave anything out.* So I try to live by these steps, and, as I said earlier, I am not a saint, so I am not perfect either, but I am trying to improve myself.

I look upon the Twelve Steps as a ladder. I have two good handrails to hang onto: the *"Serenity Prayer" and the AA unity.* But this ladder I will never reach the top of, *because nobody graduates from the program.* It seems more as if I am climbing a revolving stairway. Anyway, as long as I am on this ladder and hanging onto the railings, *I cannot fall off the ladder.* For some people this climbing might be hard, but *remember, the rungs and the railings are very solid. They will not break.*

Some people use the "Serenity Prayer" more than others, and I don't think I use it as often now as I did when I first came to the program. Try to say the "Serenity Prayer" this way:

> *God, grant me the Serenity to accept the things I cannot change—TODAY,*
> *The courage to change the things I can—TODAY,*
> *And the wisdom to know the difference—TODAY.*

Everything can be so much easier if we try *just for today,* not for a week or month from now. I cannot really plan for tomorrow, because I might not be around tomorrow. *No one knows what tomorrow will bring,* so let us make the best out of today—*the only day that is important. The only day that we have to live is today.* Yesterday is gone, and we cannot change anything we did or said, but today we can do things better than yesterday.

I'm proud to say I am an alcoholic, proud, in a way, because I have found out what was ailing me. I have found out how to live without alcohol. I am friends with a great number of people who have the same sickness as I, and we understand each other. We talk the same language. *I care about people, and people care about me, and this makes me think:* If someone is here for the first time tonight, please come back, we have a lot to offer you, if you want it. One feeling you get when you join AA is the feeling of *not being alone.*

God bless every one of you, and I wish you all happy sobriety.

"Don't be afraid to get on your knees to get on your feet."

RANDOM THOUGHTS*

(TO NEWCOMERS AND OLD-TIMERS)

Whether any of you present will get anything out of what I am about to say, I do not know, but I do know that I will, and I am very selfish in this program.

An attempt to put oneself in others' shoes is a good discipline, and, even though I have been sober a few years, I do run the risk of taking my sobriety for granted, unless I keep on reminding myself that I am new to the program every morning. I am only one drink away from a big drunk which could be my very last. It is the *first drink* that will kill me, and not the fifteenth one. So as long as I refrain from taking the first, I can't run into trouble with booze. I do believe that I could have a drink today and fool everyone around me, maybe the same tomorrow, but sooner or later I would be on a big bender.

So many have told me how confusing it is to them because they began to drink again and could *"control"* their drinking for a while, but suddenly they were again back to their old ways of drinking, *not able* to handle "just a few," and problems multiplied.

Do not be discouraged if you don't feel thoroughly at ease right off the bat. Few of us did. It takes time, and we learn slowly to practice patience. We did not become alcoholics ovenight; neither are we going to "recover" overnight. If we attend many meetings and listen to what's being said by both new and old members, the mist or the fog will leave our heads and our thinking will get clearer. We need to share our feelings with each other and thereby get a more comfortable feeling inside. There are

*From another AA talk.

many benefits that come our way. We feel better and we look better.

We can remember today what took place last night. Some of us can start putting money into savings accounts and walk around with a few bucks in our pockets. The compulsion to take a drink begins to fade. We become a little more honest with ourselves. The guilt feelings we have had begin to disappear, and our fears are going away. The AA Program is a constant self-education program, and we are never too old to learn. Perhaps more gradually, our spiritual life strengthens. We begin to face reality—life as it is—rather than as we wish it were.

There are many things we cannot change, and we can learn "to accept the things we cannot change." We find that we can speak to people more easily without being phoney about how we feel.

As these changes take place inside us, a new glow begins to grow, and this "calmness" or "peace of mind" is noticed by people around us. As the second step says: "came to believe," meaning to me that it is going to happen eventually.

It might help you, as it did me, to keep in mind that we are not giving up anything worth holding onto. On the contrary, we're getting rid of something that had begun to ruin our lives. I believe it to be important how you treat yourself. You are doing such a tremendous thing, such a fantastic change with your life, that you should allow yourself some "time out." I believe God wants us to spend just as much time having fun as being serious. He does not expect us to be in church all the time. One pitfall that we are warned about is that we should get enough rest and eat regularly. When both body and mind get tired at the same time, we can so easily talk ourselves into doing things we later will regret. With the time and money that you used to devote to liquor, you'll now be able to go to a show or play, read a few books, or do what needs to be done around the house. I feel so good at a meeting when we have a newcomer who is asking questions or telling about himself because somewhere I can find myself in his story.

When it was first suggested that I try to live my life twenty-four hours at a time, I thought, "How can that be done, knowing what had been going on for so long in my past?" I also felt that failing to plan the details of the future was a sign of poor management. However, after having given some sober consideration to this, it became clear that for me to worry about the past, with its mistakes and horrible experiences, and to worry about the future, with its promises and possible failures, was most likely more than I could carry. I am beginning to see and to understand more and more about this twenty-four hours at a time, yet I do not know it all by any means.

We are fresh to the program every day. My day begins with the same routine. I stop the alarm clock. I sit down on the edge of the bed and ask God for help and guidance for today. Today I am a potential drunk, but by the grace of God I can make a choice. Today is mine and I choose to stay sober. Today I am, as it were, brand new in a brand new world, with all its cruelty or good, but I have a choice now. Yesterdays should be yesterdays with which we have nothing to do. It is enough to know and accept that the way we lived our yesterdays has determined for us our today. And all the tomorrows should be tomorrows, with which we have nothing to do. Again, it is enough to know that the way I live today might also determine my tomorrows. I am in a life today where my thoughts have brought me, and I will be tomorrow where today's thinking takes me. So, it is important to me how I think this very moment.

If I can live, to the best of my ability, only this instant, with all its richness, its glory, its possibilities, maybe this will bring me to the realization of the highest life that can be conceived. And I have been told that there is nothing conceivable in this life that cannot be realized somehow, somewhere.

Since coming into AA, I have not had to drink; but in other ways I do my stumbling and falling. I do not feel that I have been mentally sober all the time, due to screwed-up thoughts at times. If I can learn to live each day so that when the twilight comes and night falls, I shall have lived a man's part and done a man's work in the world so that I can enjoy a comfortable sobriety, peaceful and contented. This is all possible, I know, because I have achieved some of these things. But I say again, I have not learned everything about living a day at a time. I do know more about it and how to do it today than I did the first few months or first years. I try the best I can to live this program so I can be O.K. with myself, but I believe that I cannot achieve complete honesty, complete humility, or complete peace of mind. To me, only God can be complete in anything. I can only be as honest as I am capable of being today. I am new today when I leave my bed, and I am new to this program every morning, and I hope I never forget how I ended up living before I entered into this twenty-four-hours-a-day program.

"If you feel farther away from God today than yesterday, don't make any mistakes about *Who* moved."